Divine
Visits

Becoming Masters of Light
Daren Owens

Dr. Michael Salla
exopolitics.org

ECETI Ranch

Divine
Visits

Josie Varga

4th Dimension Press ■ Virginia Beach ■ Virginia

4th Dimension Press
215 67th Street
Virginia Beach, VA 23451-2061

ISBN-13: 978-0-87604-760-6

All photographs are the property of the contributors
whose stories appear in this book.

Author Photo by Brian Allen Kasper Photography

This book is dedicated in loving memory of my wonderful friend Ray Skop, a true miracle worker, who committed his life to be of service to others. No words could accurately express how thankful I am for having had the privilege of knowing him and calling him my friend. Although I will miss him, I know he will be sending me divine visits from Heaven. May God bless you, Ray.

My heart goes out to his wife Nancy, his family, and his friends. Please know that he will always be with you. Nothing can ever break the bonds of love, not even death.

The hero is the one who kindles a great light in the world, who sets up blazing torches in the dark streets of life for men to see by. The saint is the man who walks through the dark paths of the world, himself a light.—**Felix Adler**

Table of Contents

Dr. Salla exopolitics

H. 211 exopolitics.org

H 15
C 253
J 181
K 153

83 Helen
181 Joanne
7 K
159 connie

Acknowledgments

Everything happens for a reason and nothing is without purpose. Although I had no plans to write this book, here I am today writing these heartfelt words of acknowledgment to all of you. When I first heard Toni DiBernardo's story about how a divine intervention rid her body of pancreatic cancer, I was hard at work on another book with no intention of stopping. But her story eventually led me on a quest to find other divine encounters or what I call divine visits. The rest, as they say, is history.

Toni and I met when I was writing my book *Visits from Heaven* about evidential afterlife communication. We got to know each other, and I am proud to now count her among my friends. Her story touched my heart more than words could ever express. For not only was it an affirmation of just how powerful prayer is, but it also proved to me that God and heaven are always within our reach.

Poet James Russell Lowell once said, "All God's angels come to us disguised." I must disagree here because while some angels do come to us in disguise, others do not. As you will see in this book, some most certainly make their presence known to us.

Toni helped me find stories about divine and angelic encounters for this book. For this, I will forever be grateful. Thank you, Toni, for your love and support. You are an angel here on earth.

I would also like to acknowledge all the wonderful contributors. Obviously, without them, there would be no book. Thank you all so much. Your stories of divine love will change lives by helping others realize that they have access to the angelic and divine realm at all times.

Some time ago, a contributor to my book *Visits from Heaven* put me in touch with Cassie McQuagge of A.R.E. Press in order for me to obtain reprint permission. I felt an instant connection to Cassie and knew in my heart that I was meant to go with A.R.E. This book is my fourth title with them, and I am extremely grateful for their continued faith in me.

Thank you to my editor, Stephanie Pope. Her support, expertise, and friendship have been invaluable to me. To Jennie Taylor Martin, Alison Ray, and the rest of the A.R.E. crew, thank you for believing in me. I would especially like to thank A.R.E.'s CEO and Executive Director Kevin Todeschi for his support. I am extremely humbled and honored that he wrote the Foreword for this book. Thank you, Kevin.

Over the years I have gained the support of so many experts in the field. For this I am very grateful. Thank you, John L. Turner, MD, for writing the Preface. I am so deeply touched by your kind words.

I cannot end this without first acknowledging my family and friends. I am very blessed to have so many earth angels in my life. To my mother and father, I love you. To my brother Michael and sister Virginia, thank you for continuing to look after your little sister. In memory of my Godmother Lucy, thank you for paying me a special divine visit and letting me know that you are still around.

To my beautiful daughters, Erica Ann and Lia Josephine, I thank God for you every day. To John, my wonderful husband, only God and his angels could have brought together a love like ours. I love you so much.

Lastly, I want to acknowledge my friends, both old and new. Thank you for knowing me and loving me anyway. I am so blessed. Without you, my life would not be complete.

Foreword

Perhaps more than anything else, the most compelling premise presented in Josie Varga's *Divine Visits* is the fact that God in spirit can and does impact things physical. To be sure, there are times when the demands of life numb us to the ever-present reality of the Divine, but God never leaves us. It is only our awareness and consciousness that have erred and shifted in perception. The variety of ways in which people have encountered divine messengers, helpers, guides, mentors, and supporters should give us all hope in our own lives and an understanding that spirit cares and is very much cognizant of each and every one of us. We are not alone; we are never alone.

What may be surprising to a number of readers is the frequency with which divine visits occur in people's everyday lives. Whether it is Carolyn's story of her face-to-face encounter with a guardian angel during a blizzard or Lisa's experience with the consciousness of the Other Side during a heightened meditation or Uva, who was in reality an angel in disguise that assisted a family in need, these stories paint the image of a divine world very much concerned with the affairs of humankind.

The regularity of this phenomenon of divine visits resulted in my own book *God in Real Life: Personal Encounters with the Divine* a number of years ago as people from every imaginable walk of life and religious (and non-religious) background sought me out with a story that frequently began, "You are never going to believe what I am about to tell you . . . " But the truth is there are countless stories of how this phenomenon can and does happen and numerous examples of how even the most skeptical can't help but believe after having divine visitors of their own.

Collected here are stories that hold true to the biblical claim that oftentimes individuals who have encountered (the Bible uses the phrase "entertained") strangers have entertained angels unaware. (Hebrews 13:2) This same assertion was echoed by famed psychic Edgar Cayce when he told individuals to become aware of how they treated one another: " . . . be ye mindful in every association and manner when ye entertain strangers, for often ye entertain angels unawares. (520-3)" In this wonderful volume there are a startling number of divine visits collected for easy reflection and contemplation. This fact caused me to wonder—as Cayce suggested—just how many divine visits forever remain unrecognized. In our own lives, how often have we entertained angels and divine messengers without becoming conscious of what truly transpired?

I had personally heard of literally dozens of divine encounters from all kinds of individuals before encountering one for myself. Although I truly believed the stories I was hearing, it was only after my own experience that I understood the depth of meaning that these encounters have for individuals firsthand. For a number of years I was very close to a woman named Angela Marsh Peterson. Angela lived for ninety-eight years and had a very full life. An amazing woman from many different perspectives, Angela's life included many of the possible experiences available to a woman in the twentieth century: motherhood, career, travel, the military, owning her own business, divorce, the death of a child, founding her own museum, teaching, serving as a house mother to college students, living overseas; the list goes on and on. Because of her incredibly varied life, Angela had been encouraged on, at least, a dozen different occasions to compile her life's story. Although there were numerous attempts, the story was never completed. Then Angela and I met, and something clicked. For more than four years we worked on her story, which was eventually published as *One Woman's Century*. Although Angela never lived to see the book in print, she did read all but the last thirty pages or so.

About one year after Angela's death, I was asleep, or so I thought, and I had a dream. In the dream I was slumbering in the bed; the lights were off. I could see myself, the room, the bed, and a flicker of moonlight through the window. All at once, as though bathed in bright light, Angela appeared in the bedroom. She was smiling, energetic, and no longer crippled over with her ninety-eight years. She thanked me for finishing the book, leaned over, and gave me a very brief kiss on the lips. As soon as her lips touched mine, it was like being shot full of electricity! I sat up immediately in bed, wide awake, fully conscious, and very much aware that I had just had a divine encounter of my own. Not only had Angela come to give thanks but her presence reassured me because at that time I was losing one of my very best friends to cancer. The Divine in spirit is interested with the concerns of the material world.

On a number of occasions, Edgar Cayce told stories of his own divine encounters throughout the years. Those experiences began when he was less than two years old and had "invisible playmates" that he eventually recognized as young children who had passed away and were not quite ready to move on to the next experience in consciousness. As a young boy, he had an encounter with an angelic woman to whom he told his dream to be helpful to people, "especially children when they were sick." She acknowledged the dream, promised it would be answered, and then disappeared. As an adult and an accomplished speaker, Cayce occasionally had the experience of lecturing to a room of people and becoming aware of the fact that "invisible people" would come in and take seats where no one was sitting in order to listen to what was being said.

I believe that these stories give credence to the ever-present reality of the Divine in our lives. Sometimes they come in the form of chance encounters. Sometimes they are the flicker of a dream or a simple divine insight. Sometime they are an angel that we entertain unaware. Sometimes all we have to do is look beyond ourselves and we will find the very thing we need. But the fact is that the Divine is very much cognizant of us; perhaps the time has come, at last, for us to become cognizant in return.

Kevin J. Todeschi
Executive Director and CEO
Edgar Cayce's A.R.E./Atlantic University
EdgarCayce.org

Preface

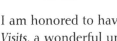

I am honored to have been asked to comment on Josie Varga's *Divine Visits*, a wonderful undertaking which provides real-life stories of extraordinary individuals who have experienced a divine intervention in the form of visitations by guardian spirits and angels. My work as a physicist and neurological surgeon has inexorably led me to the study of after-death communication, the existence of the afterlife, and the importance and function of guardian angels. On my office desk sits a glass 3D sculpture of German painter Bernhard Plockhorst's *Schutzengel*. It shows two children being protected by a guardian angel as they cross a damaged footbridge. For the past year, as patients describe their automobile accidents, I let them see and hold this small piece of art. Almost to a person, they report the awareness of some sort of divine intervention at the time of their injury. Some have described the vehicle being steered or moved by unseen forces. It is quite interesting to see that this is almost universal in cases of serious and life-threatening injuries. This has helped me to understand that everything happens for a purpose and that there are no coincidences.

The history of the Catholic Church shows that the *Feast of the Dedication of St. Michael* is among the oldest feasts, and as part of it, there was a tribute to the angels with an acknowledgment of their protective office and intercessory power. Angels have been with us, well described in the literature, and I will venture to say that at some point in one's life, the appreciation of guardians and angels begins to shine like a beacon as we awaken to the existence of the afterlife. In this fifth work by Josie Varga, the topic of divine intervention is covered from many different viewpoints. According to the author of this fascinating book, "Life never ends and love never dies, and that nothing can break the bonds of love—not even death." There is a love expressed in these stories of interventions which comes in various sizes, hues, appearances, and races. They are anecdotal stories indeed, but what faith can we place in them?

I was privileged to be one of the keynote speakers at the *First International Conference on After-Death Communication* in Phoenix, AZ, April 2012. I concluded my first presentation on the afterlife with a mention of Dr. Michael Newton's *Journey of Souls* and the importance of examining the time-between-lives. I met author Robert Schwartz, author of *Your Soul's Plan: Discovering the Real Meaning of the Life You Planned before You Were Born*, who also writes about the period between lives. One thing is clear from their work and that of many others: *All of us have guardian angels and guides.* We need to understand and to fully appreciate how the process of divine intervention works. One day we, too, will appreciate such intervention. That is where this book is very helpful—it shows us how divine visits occur.

Do we need to call on the angels or will they simply show up when their intervention is necessary? Well, it depends. You will learn about the subtle ways in which they might make their presence known. You will also learn of the stupendous ways in which forces that seemingly violate the laws of physics are brought into play with lifesaving results. You will also read about cases in which calls are put forth and the angels promptly respond.

After reading this book, you will appreciate the fact that there is ample evidence to suggest that there is an afterlife and that angels appear when needed. They come when called upon and can assist without being asked. This wonderful book contains numerous stories of angelic visitations—all inspiring in their own right; however, the author's own angelic visitation as she lay on the radiology table, visually seeing and interacting with the *orb*, will move you. My eyes filled with tears of joy and understanding as I read her description of this life-saving event in the chapter "Beyond Words." You will find the pages of this book filled with tales of total love and compassion. With knowledge, fear tends to dissipate. Please enjoy your read.

John L. Turner, MD
Author of *Medicine, Miracles, and Manifestations: A Doctor's Journey through the Worlds of Divine Intervention, Near-Death Experiences, and Universal Energy.*
www.JohnLTurner.com

Introduction

> For God commands the angels to guard you in all your ways.
>
> With their hands they shall support you, lest you strike your foot
> against a stone.   **Psalms 91:11-12**

The word angel is derived from the word *angelos* which means messenger in Greek. Angels, those spiritual beings who perform God's will, appear everywhere in the Bible from the book of Genesis all the way to the book of Revelation. In Luke 22:43 angels announce the birth of Jesus, and in John 20:12 they proclaim his resurrection from the dead. What some may not realize, however, is that the Bible even notes when angels sometimes take human form.

When a son is promised to Abraham in Genesis 18:1–3 (NRSV), three men suddenly appear. "The Lord appeared to Abraham by the oaks of Mamre as he sat at the entrance of his tent in the heat of the day. He looked up and saw three men standing near him. When he saw them, he ran from the tent entrance to meet them, and bowed to the ground. He said, 'My Lord, if I find favour with you, do not pass by your servant.'"

Saint Thomas Aquinas was a great medieval theologian who was often referred to as the Angelic Doctor because he spent a lot of time talking and writing about angels. He believed that not only were angels spiritual beings who could take on any form but that they were also highly intellectual beings.

We all have angels who are there to help us and lead us in the right direction so that our soul can learn and grow in love. However, he also said that for this to happen we have to want to be led. So, in other words, they are there to assist us at any time as long as we desire their assistance because we still have free will.

In the 1998 film *City of Angels*, an angel named Seth (Nicholas Cage) falls in love with a beautiful heart surgeon (Meg Ryan) and must choose between his heavenly duties or his earthly desires. In one of the scenes from the movie, Dr. Maggie Rice is upset about the death of her patient and says, "He should have lived." To this Seth says, "He is living. Just not the way you think." The doctor then replies, "I don't . . . believe in . . . that."

The angel then looks at the doctor and says, "Some things are true whether you believe them or not." That line has stayed with me ever since. So true! Think of it this way, say you consider yourself to be an agnostic or an atheist, does this affect whether God or angels are or aren't a reality? No, it does not. The truth is the truth regardless of what you believe.

More than half of all Americans believe in the existence of angels according to a 2008 survey conducted by Baylor University's Institute for Studies of Religion which polled 1,700 respondents. I have no doubt that the percentage is much higher these days. What I find particularly interesting is that one in five of those surveyed who claimed that they were not religious still believed that they were protected in some way and at some point in life by angels.

St. Thomas held that the failure of some to believe in angels was due to the fact that many people are quick to write off the presence of spirits or angels as mere imagination. They can't, he noted, tell the difference between what they are imagining and what they are truly sensing. If we could tell the difference, then we would know without a doubt that we are always in the presence of angels.

Angels, he also believed, influence mankind by putting thoughts in our head and giving us ideas. We may not even realize it at the time, but our very thoughts may be divinely guided.

In addition to putting thoughts in our head, angels can also posit pictures in our mind. I can say without hesitation that this is true because I was lucky enough to experience a divine intervention like this myself. On Memorial Day 2011, I decided to go to the local Target store and run some errands.

After about an hour, I exited the store with my full cart and headed to my car. All of a sudden in a quick instant I saw a vision of myself getting hit by a car and felt all of the emotions of my family and friends. I knew I was killed by this car though I didn't see myself dead. It was so powerful and immediate that I stopped in my tracks and sort of did a double take wondering what the heck had just happened. I stopped for about five seconds trying to shake it off and then pro-ceeded to push my cart to my car.

All of a sudden a man, driving a pickup truck, backed up out of a spot directly in front of me without looking. He pulled out so fast that I quickly reached forward and pulled my cart back. If I hadn't, he would have hit my cart full on. I stood there, out of breath, clutching my cart, and staring at the man in the truck who looked at me in shock, knowing he had come so close to killing me. He looked at me apologetically, put his truck back in drive, and pulled back into his spot. My heart was still racing as I watched him put his truck in park and then bury his face in his hands.

Looking back I don't know why I didn't go up to this man; perhaps it was the shock of the whole ordeal. As he sat there, I'm sure contem-plating how he could have killed me; I was actually thinking, *OH MY GOD, I saw this happen before it happened.* I felt no anger for this stranger, only compassion sensing how bad he felt.

When I finally got back to my car and drove home, I was numb and shell shocked wondering how I was going to tell my husband what had just transpired. When I did, his eyes watered thinking of the un-thinkable. But I couldn't help but wonder why this had happened to me. Why had I been shown this vision? Why had my life been spared?

The following week I was talking to a friend of mine (who is a medium) and told him what happened. "Josie," he said, "that was your spirit guide sending you that message. Had you not listened and stopped, you would have been killed. I am so glad you listened." Although intuitively I already knew this, it was hard to hear.

Had I not listened, I would not be here today to share this story with you (at least not in the physical). But the truth is I would not be here even more so had it not been for the spirit who sent me that message or vision in the first place. My friend called this spirit a spirit guide. To me, in addition to being my spirit guide, this spirit was also an angel.

People have often asked me what I think the difference is between an angel and a spirit guide. And before I can answer this, I need to first mention Saint Augustine, the Catholic saint and mystic. According to this extraordinary man, "Angels are spirits, but it is not because they are spirits that they are angels. They become angels when they are sent. For the name angel refers to their office, not their nature. You ask the name of this nature, it is spirit; you ask its office, it is that of an Angel."[1]

As I said earlier, the word angel is of Greek origin meaning messenger. So I find St. Augustine's explanation of angels to be very interesting. For one thing we are all spirit. Spirit is our true nature; we are not the body. But St. Augustine pointed out that it is not this nature that makes them angels but their office, which another way of saying what they do or the message they portray.

I believe that a person is an angel because of his deeds and not his nature. Having said this, I believe that spirit guides are different levels of angels. You have the highest level which includes the Archangels Gabriel and Michael all the way to spirits who once walked among us on this earth and now work to help people still in human form. All are sent to us to help us with our journey or purpose here on earth.

They help us, for example, by sending us signs. You see someone's name or hear it on four different occasions on the same day. They may be putting this person in your mind so that you contact him. Other times we may have a feeling about something or even hear a voice in our head. When I was about twenty-one, I was driving home as an icy mist covered the roadways. I found myself on a normally busy street in my hometown of Elizabeth, New Jersey when without warning I

---

[1] www.catholictradition.org/Angels/angels1.htm

lost control of my car as it began to skid on the ice. My initial thought was to try to turn my steering wheel away from the direction of the parked cars and the utility pole, but suddenly I heard a voice say, "Let go of the wheel." I quickly let go and just sat in my vehicle as the car continued to skid as if it had a mind of its own. I think I must have said a bunch of "Hail Mary's" and "Our Fathers" in mere seconds before my car came to a halt within about a foot from the utility pole.

We've all heard this little intuitive voice at one time or another during our lives; however most of us just dismiss it as a figure of our imagination. The angels and spirit guides can guide us by bringing certain people into our lives. How many times have you met someone and had the feeling that you were meant to meet him? Chances are you were.

Part of the Nicene Creed reads:

> We believe in one God,
> the Father, the Almighty
> maker of heaven and earth,
> of all that is, seen and unseen.

Although angels and spirit guides are part of this unseen (spirit) existence, sometimes they do make themselves seen for our benefit. In fact, as you will realize in this book, often times we need only to ask for their help and it will be given. Hopefully after reading the divine visits which follow you will know, without a doubt, that we are never really alone. There is always someone watching over us.

You Are Healed

It is only fitting that I begin with the heartwarming story which gave me the idea for this book. I met Toni DiBernardo when she contacted me with a story for my book *Visits from Heaven*, which was released in December 2009. The story, ironically entitled *My Brother Joey, the Angel*, tells of an afterlife communication or visit from heaven her mother experienced when Toni's deceased brother Joey appeared at her death-bed.

She writes, "The week that my mother died, I had experiences that were just unbelievable as she was communicating with my father and brother Joey who had already passed. One day my mother looked at me and told me that my brother Joey was in the room with us. She said, 'Oh, I wish that you could see this beautiful male angel all dressed in white. I'm afraid if you turn your head too fast, he will leave; he is so beautiful.'"

She went on as if she were having a conversation with this angel. "Did you hear what he just told me?" she asked. Then without waiting for an answer she continued, "I told him to please put me down because I was going to make him fall and he told me, 'Mom, I won't let you fall. You are as light as these feathers on my back.'" I couldn't believe what I was hearing. She then looked at me and said, "Toni, it's Joey; I always knew he was an angel."

Years later Toni experienced her own divine visit. Only this time, it was not her brother or anyone else in her family. This time she says she was visited by Jesus himself. I will never forget the day when Toni called to tell me that she had just been diagnosed with pancreatic cancer. She was understandably very upset and wasn't sure if she wanted to even go through with the recommended surgery to remove the tumor along with part of her pancreas and spleen.

At that time, she wondered if she should even bother having the surgery. Pancreatic cancer has one of the lowest survival rates with less than 5 percent of those diagnosed reaching the five-year mark. Part of the problem is the fact that this cancer is very rarely diagnosed early enough because there are typically no symptoms early on.

Toni Di Bernardo

During the later stages of the disease, symptoms include jaundice and abdominal pain.

That day as we spoke on the phone I could totally understand why Toni had her doubts about having the surgery. However, I encouraged her to go through with the surgery. In my mind, it was better to at least fight the cancer, and her family felt so as well.

Luckily, Toni opted to have the surgery, and I told her that she would, of course, be in my prayers. I went over to the local Target and purchased a figurine of a cross and sent it to her in support. Prior to mailing it to her, I said a prayer asking God to please help her. Unbeknownst to me, Toni would later take this cross to the hospital with her. During this time prior to the surgery, Toni's friend Ruthie, who is very religious, put a prayer shawl on Toni and recited what is known as simply the Jewish Prayer. The following is the prayer in both Hebrew and English:

> *Baruch Ata Adonai*
> **Blessed Art thou Our Lord**
> *Malki Ot Haolam*
> **King of the Universe**
> *Shama Adonai Elohay*
> **Hear me oh Lord my God**
> *Shiva atiele Cha va Tiypaenee*
> **I cried to thee and thou hast healed me.**
> *Ahalela Shem Elohim*
> **I will praise thy name, O God**
> *Kooma Adonai*
> **Arise, O Lord**
> *Hoshieynee Elohay*
> **Save me, O my God**
> *In Yeshua Shem Kodesh*
> **Jesus Holy Name, Amen.**

After reciting the above prayer, Ruthie used some holy oil imported from Jerusalem to make the sign of the cross on Toni's forehead. Immediately afterward, Toni began to feel hot and told her friend how she was feeling. To this Ruthie excitedly replied, "That usually doesn't happen, Toni. You are healed."

A week later, Toni went in for the surgery and spent a long time recuperating. After two months, she had an appointment with her oncologist to be rechecked to see where she stood with the cancer. The tests would determine, for instance, if removal of the tumor had in fact removed the cancer or if the disease was still progressing. While they

Toni's picture of Jesus in her home

were waiting for the results, she told the doctor that she wanted to thank the people who had helped her in the hospital and asked for the name of one particular doctor. Here's what happened: She was in her hospital room recovering and remembers being woken up. She then opened her eyes and remembers thinking: *I must be dead* and closed her eyes again. She was awoken a second time and again reasoned she was dead and closed her eyes. The third time she felt a warm tap on her shoulder and woke up. Before her, she said, was a man who looked like he was wearing a white doctor's coat. She looked at him and said she immediately thought he resembled Jesus in a picture she has hanging in her home.   At this point, for some reason, she asked him what nationality he was. His response was, "I am Israeli Jew." To this, Toni replied, "You have the most beautiful eyes I have ever seen."

The man then bent down and kissed her twice on the forehead saying, "You are healed." This is all that she can remember.

So this day at the oncologist's office, she wanted the name of the man with the beautiful eyes so that she could thank him. Totally unprepared for the response, Toni was told that there was no such doctor. There was no "Israeli Jew" that fit her description. Toni was absolutely stunned. What's more? The tests results came back, and Toni was told that there was no sign of cancer. Her astonished doctor remarked, "Go home and pretend you never had cancer."

When Toni called me to tell me what had happened, I was ecstatic and shocked all at the same time. I felt almost like I had experienced it myself in some way as happy tears filled my eyes. A week later I was scheduled to speak during a conference in Virginia Beach at the Association for Research and Enlightenment (A.R.E.). I asked Toni if she would mind if I shared her beautiful story with the audience. My point in telling Toni's story was for the audience to understand the definite power of prayer. As I relayed the story, I noticed a woman who seemed to be listening to me intently. When my speech concluded, people lined up to have me sign copies of my books. It was then that I noticed the attentive woman purposely standing in the back. When the line died down, she slowly walked up to me. She started to say something, but her eyes soon welled up with tears. I immediately walked from behind the table and gave her a hug asking her to tell me what was wrong.

"Josie," she told me, "You know that story you told before about the woman with cancer?" I nodded that I did indeed remember. "I feel like that was a sign for me," she explained, "I was just diagnosed with breast cancer, and your story has given me hope." Tears filled my own eyes as I hugged her again. We just never know how our actions will affect others. It was then that I knew that this story was meant to be told and realized if I could help this woman, then I could surely help others. Hence, this book was born.

I read the chapter ahead of time. During the reading in group I found my self going into a "sleep" hearing words w/out recognition of meaning, but feeling a healing effect. This has happened Before. It's like a "required" slow down and let the Divine do what is needed.

Beyond Words

─────··◄◅∞►▻··─────

As I often say, there are no coincidences in life; there are only "Godincidences." Nearing the completion of this book, I experienced my own profound divine visit. As I write these words, I am overcome with emotion just thinking about it. And although the experience is beyond words, I will do my best to describe what happened.

In March 2012 I had an appointment for my annual mammogram. Shortly after I was told that I needed to go back for another scan. Typically this does not alarm me as I have dense breasts and, therefore, very often have to go back for a second mammogram or ultrasound. This time, however, they needed to take another look at the left side of my breasts.

Since I was traveling, I could not make an appointment until two weeks later which brought me back for a screening on Monday, April 9th–a day that I will remember vividly for the rest of my life. When I arrived, I was first given another mammogram by one of the x-ray technicians on staff. Afterwards I was told that the doctor wanted me to have an ultrasound. At this point I must admit I was concerned but not alarmed.

As the second technician scanned my breasts, I noticed that she paid special attention to one area on the left side. After she spent several minutes examining the scans of my breasts, she looked at me and said, "I'll be right back. I have to go talk to the doctor." As she left the room leaving me alone with my thoughts, I sensed that I was in trouble. My body literally began to shake from head to toe.

Not knowing what else to do, I decided to ask God if everything was going to be okay. I was hoping that my gut instincts were wrong so I asked telepathically, *Is everything okay?* Unexpectedly and shockingly, I clearly heard a voice in my mind say, *No!* You can just imagine how shocked I was. At this point I thought maybe I had imagined it and asked again, *Is everything okay?* Again I unmistakably heard back, *No!*

Honestly, I wanted to run out of that room. I was startled, confused, scared, etc. There I was lying on a table, topless in a dimly lit room alone. Not knowing what else to do, I cried out to God for help. I was so distraught that I cannot remember my exact words, but they went something like this: *Well, God, if it's not okay, you have to fix this. I can't leave yet. I'm doing so much right now. I need to finish my book. Lord, I want to be there for my children.* Then holding back tears, I thought of my Godmother Lucy. Let me pause here and give you a little description of my beautiful, wonderful godmother Lucy LoBrace.

Lucy was the type of person who always put everyone before herself. She did everything she could to help everyone else and never thought much about her own needs. She never married and worked as a seamstress for several years at a company in Elizabeth, New Jersey. Since she had no children, I was her self-proclaimed daughter, and I proudly called her my second mom. We passed many hours together as I grew up, going shopping downtown, having sleepovers, or just passing time lounging on her big Victorian porch. As we both grew older, the bond we shared grew stronger, and I cherished the times I got to spend with Lucy.

I could go on and on talking about what a wonderful person she was, but what's important here is that she had more faith in God than anyone I have ever known. Despite many hardships in her life and through the untimely death of many of her close family members, she held on to her faith. She strongly believed in the power of prayer and kept a shrine of saint medallions in her room: St. Jude, St. Joseph, and St. Theresa. She had them all. She also faithfully said many daily novenas to various saints and when she was physically able, always attended mass on Sundays.

Through the years I would always tell her, "Lucy, if there's anyone who is going to get to heaven, it's you. Put in a good word for me when you get there." She would always just smile at me and chuckle. I would also tell her to make sure that she gave me a sign to let me know that everything was okay when she crossed over. Lucy unexpectedly passed on February 22, 2010 from an apparent heart attack. Although I was shocked and saddened by the news, I had no doubt whatsoever that she was in a much better place and was now happy to be with her loved ones once again. In fact, she has let me know in many ways that she is still with me. I will share one example here before I get back to that day in the radiology room.

Often when I'm at my desk writing, I go onto You Tube and put in a song that I can listen to as I write. Recently I was really missing my Godmother Lucy and put "My Melody of Love" in the search field. For those of you who may not know, this was a popular song by singer Bobby Vinton in the 70s.

When I was young, my godmother gave me a Mickey Mouse record player. It was white with Mickey Mouse on the cover, and the needle was actually Mickey's arm. I loved it, and it brought me many hours of enjoyment. One day Lucy came over with the 45 of "My Melody of Love," and the two of us had such a great time doing the polka and singing to this Bobby Vinton hit.

So on this day as I sat there missing my godmother, I wanted to hear this song that had special meaning to both of us. As the song played via You Tube, the tears began to flow. Suddenly I yelled out as if she was within earshot, "Lucy, are you here? Do you remember this? Bobby Vinton. "My Melody of Love?" I then cried for several more minutes before going back to my work.

The following week, my husband John asked me if my daughter Lia had told me about the dream she had had involving my godmother. When I told him that she hadn't, he told me to ask her what happened. When I did, Lia seemed confused and flustered. She told me that she had had a dream about "Grandma Lucy" (this is what my two

daughters called Lucy) but was confused by it. I told her to just tell me
what happened, and this is what she said:

> Mommy, Grandma Lucy walked up to this box and opened it.
> When she opened it, there was this thing going round and round
> and there was a little stick sticking up.

I stood there open mouthed. My daughter Lia unknowingly just
gave me a huge validation. I realized that Lia was, of course, describing a record player, but Lia was ten years old. So in this age of CDs and
MP3 players, she had no idea of what she was seeing. She is not familiar with LPs and 45s. She is not familiar with record players. So why,
then, did she dream of my godmother and a record player? This was
Lucy's way of letting me know that she did remember. Yes, she was
there, and yes, she did remember "My Melody of Love."

By the way, I showed my daughter pictures of record players, and
she confirmed that this was what she had indeed seen. But why would
my Godmother Lucy visit my daughter in a dream and not me? This is
what is called a third-party sign. Think about it for a moment. Obviously, it is more validating for my Godmother Lucy to go to my daughter Lia and not to me. I may have thought I was having the dream
simply because I had asked Lucy if she was there with me. However,
hearing this message from Lia (a third party who had no knowledge of
what happened) was a far stronger and convincing validation.

As I said earlier, Lucy has given me many signs or visits from heaven
as I like to call them such as the one I just described above, but everything pales in comparison to what happened that day as I waited for
the technician to return. Again, I had cried out to God telepathically
for help and then thought of my godmother. So I decided to make a
second plea for help to Lucy.

"Lucy," I pleaded. "If I've ever needed you to be here for me, it's now.
Please, Lucy, help me!"

And then it happened. Within mere seconds I saw a bright white
orb descend from the ceiling directly above me. I stared at it in utter
astonishment and thought, *I must be imagining things.* I closed my eyes
and opened them again, but it was still there. The white was very
bright, and it was not transparent. In other words, I could not see

through this orb which looked to be about four inches long and just three inches wide. The orb was perfectly round but had rays of light protruding out of it.

No doubt something very divine was taking place. I lay there mesmerized by this beautiful, breathtaking vision and watched as it slowly descended toward me. A smile warmed my face, and I completely calmed down. When the orb came to about four inches above my chest, it then slowly moved to my right and stopped.

At this point I communicated with this divine presence telepathically saying, *It's okay. I'm not afraid; come to me*, and reached out my hand to it. When I did, the orb slowly turned a beautiful, vibrant purple. For lack of a better description, the orb looked to be alive with energy and vibration. A small dot of purple formed in the center and then became bigger and bigger until it encompassed most of the white, changing color right before my eyes. As though I was in a trance, I lay there spellbound watching what was unfolding before me, feeling totally at peace and content. Then . . . the technician suddenly opened the door. My heart skipped a beat as she broke my trance, and the magnificent orb quickly disappeared, leaving me wishing that the technician had given me more time to take in this divine visit.

As she took more scans of my breasts, my mind and my heart were elsewhere as I replayed over and over again in my mind what had just happened to me. I wondered how I was going to explain to my family and friends what had just occurred to me. I even wondered if they would believe me but then quickly decided that it didn't matter who believed and who did not believe. I knew what had happened, and that's all that mattered. But as I drove home that day, I couldn't help but wonder what it all meant. Was it God? Was it my Godmother Lucy? Was I being told that everything was going to be okay? Or was I being told that it was my time but not to worry? And why had the orb turned purple? What did this all mean?

When my husband returned home from work later that day, I told him what had happened as he looked at me dumbfounded by my words. "That is amazing!" he said. "That is a once in a lifetime experience. Just incredible! What a blessing!"

Yes, it was a blessing, but I couldn't help but ponder why it happened. Who came to me and why? As an author and researcher of the afterlife and the paranormal, I certainly had no qualms about what I saw. It was clearly an orb which is how spirit energy often manifests in photographs. But there is a big difference between seeing an orb in a photo and seeing one in person while totally awake! There is also a big difference between being visited by spirits or deceased loved ones during your dream state and actually seeing them with your own eyes.

Two days later I answered the phone to hear my gynecologist on the other end. "Josephine, there is something on your left side. There is something there that shouldn't be there. I want you to have a biopsy as soon as possible. Don't wait."

I could clearly hear the panic in his voice. He referred me to a breast cancer specialist and told me to make an appointment. Everything goes blank from that moment on because I was so stunned that I couldn't hear the rest of my doctor's words. I do remember hanging up the phone and crying. I had been through this all before when I was diagnosed with melanoma in 2000. I had gotten the same call. I had heard the same panic. All those painful memories came rushing back. Only now I had two beautiful young daughters to worry about.

Why? Why would this happen to me in the midst of everything that I am trying to do to get the word out about God, the power of prayer, the afterlife, universal consciousness, etc. Mostly, however, I kept thinking about my kids. As I've said in my books many times, I am not afraid to die. The body is just a garment we wear in order to be able to experience life on this earth. When we crossover, we change our outfit. We go back to being spirit which is and always will be our true essence. Because I know this, it is definitely easier for me when I lose a loved one, but it's definitely not easy. It hurts. It really hurts. I am only human so I long for that physical contact just like everyone else.

Two days later I attended an engagement party for my neighbor's daughter. In all honesty I did not want to go because I was upset and worried, but I didn't want to cancel at the last minute either. So my husband and I put on a happy face and tried to make the best of it. It was a beautiful affair, and I ended up sitting next to my neighbor and friend Janet, who is a breast cancer survivor. I hadn't planned on talking about my predicament but decided to ask Janet for her advice.

After I told her about my hectic week, she looked at me surprisingly and said, "It's you!" I had no idea what she was talking about, but she went on to explain that she had had a vivid dream. In the dream she was told that someone was going to be coming to her for help. "Josie," she said, "It's you. You are the one that I am supposed to help!" WOW! I looked at her both astonished and grateful as I knew someone was looking after me on the Other Side. Janet went on to tell me that what made this even more astonishing was that she usually never remembers her dreams. But she had had no doubt she was meant to remember this one.

The following week I went to see the breast specialist who examined me and set up an appointment for a biopsy. While I waited for the day of the biopsy, I tried to keep myself busy with writing this book. One day as I was going over one of the chapters, I froze when I came to Lori's response to one of my questions. Lori, who is a gifted psychic medium, wrote, "We humans are made up of matter, and matter is energy. Energy can neither be created, nor can it be destroyed. When we die, the energy is still there and takes a new form. If you were to see it, you would see hazy smoke or orbs of light." I read this and reread this. " . . . you would see hazy smoke or orbs of light."

I then wrote to Lori telling her what had happened to me at the imaging center. In response she wrote, "When you called on your godmother to be with you, she was. You pulled down a wall and invited a loved one in. You were open, and she presented to you." I was just stunned as I read her words. So it really was my Godmother Lucy! Lori also went on to explain that the reason the orb changed colors is because when I reached out to it, my energy fused with my godmother's energy, thereby creating the color purple.

Lori concluded, "You have love on your side." I can't tell you how much her comforting words had meant to me. I have a wonderful page on Facebook based on my book *Visits from Heaven*.[2] I have told the bereaved countless times that their loved ones are just a thought away. "When we think of our loved ones, we bring them to us. If you need help, just ask. They can be of more help to us from the Other Side than they were when they were on this Earth." I have said these words so

---

[2]For information about the *Visits from Heaven* Facebook Group or to join, please visit: https://www.facebook.com/groups/256369014386004/.

many times, and now I experienced the truth of my very own words. I was desperate for help. I cried out to God. I asked my Godmother Lucy for help. Within seconds she manifested before me in the form of an orb. She was always there for me and still is. Only now Lucy is in spirit.

A few days later, I had the biopsy and the stressful wait for the results began. The biopsy was performed on Tuesday, April 24. Two days later my phone rang early in the morning. It was the breast imaging doctor on the line. "It is benign," he said. "I just read the report and had to call you. I am surprised. I thought it was cancer." He went on to say how it had looked like cancer to him, but I don't remember his exact words because my happy sobs kept interrupting him.

"No, I'm telling you this because you should be happy," he quickly added trying to calm me. I remember uttering something like, "I know. Thank you." How was I going to explain what had happened in that room to this doctor? How was I going to tell him that I believed my fate was changed in that very room when the orb appeared before me? I hung up the phone and continued sobbing in my husband John's arms.

The doctor's honesty confirmed what I had been feeling all along and what I was told that day. Remember, I had asked God telepathically, *Is everything okay?* And I clearly heard back in my mind, *No!* I asked this same question twice, and twice I heard, *No!* Why would I hear back, *No,* if everything was alright? Why would I hear this if it wasn't cancer? Why would I hear this if it was originally benign?

Fast forward another week and I was in my gynecologist/obstetrician's office for my annual exam. We talked about the biopsy, and since I have a close relationship with my ob–gyn, I decided to tell him what had transpired that day at the diagnostic center. I also told him that I knew it didn't look good because the imaging doctor had told me he thought it was cancer.

My doctor then admitted that this is what was reported to him. "Listen, I don't know what happened here," he told me. "Let's just be happy with the results." He went on to say that he often hears stories such as mine and that there are things in life we just can't explain.

While I agree that there are some things in life that we just can't explain, I don't believe that this experience is one of them. I know that what happened to me on that day in that room was a divine intervention. I also know that the power of prayer played a huge part in my good fortune. Many family and friends were praying for me, including rosary groups. I was saying daily novenas to the Blessed Mother, Saint Peregrine, and Padre Pio. In fact, the day after I was told that I needed to have a biopsy, I was in my room praying to my Godmother Lucy. A few minutes later I went into my drawer looking for a prayer card she had given me. I found the card along with a note from my godmother. In it I found a small medal depicting the Blessed Mother. As I read the note, I was stunned when I came to the last paragraph. In it, she wrote, "Pin this medal on your bra. It's blessed."

Rereading the note, I stared in disbelief. "Pin this medal on your bra." My godmother once again came to me with a message of her presence at the most opportune time. I said a prayer of thanks and then took the medal and pinned it to the left side of my bra. That same night I called my friend Ray Skop, a faith healer in Jersey City, New Jersey, who has been at the helm of several miracles. (We will talk more about Ray a little later in this book).

So while many factors played a part in my positive outcome and I cannot possibly exempt anything while expressing my thanks, I can say that it all began with the divine visit that I received in that room at the diagnostic radiology center. I can also say it began with my desperate cry for help and hence the appearance and miracle of that incredible orb.

My life hasn't been the same since. I am a new person. The sky is bluer. The grass is greener. Everything radiates with love and energy. When I called Toni DiBernardo whose divine visit I described in the previous chapter and who assisted me in putting this book together, she excitedly exclaimed, "I know exactly what you mean, Josie. I call these God Shots. Everything looks more beautiful than it did before." I smiled in agreement feeling and sharing in her excitement. I wasn't alone in my newfound way of looking at the world. While Toni prefers to call it God Shots, I like to think of it more as soul impressions for I no longer see with my eyes; I see with my soul. And while mere words don't begin to describe the magnificence of what I experienced that day, at least I have given you a glimpse.

Uva

Bibiana
California

Times were tough. At this time in my life I had five children, all under the age of ten, and I was pregnant with my sixth child. We were living and hiding from my brutal ex-husband in an old house that was scheduled to be demolished, and therefore, thankfully, I paid no rent.

Various caring family members and friends would stop by every now and then to bring the children and me a bag of potatoes, some vegetables, or eggs since I couldn't collect the court-ordered child support money from my husband and risk uncovering our whereabouts.

One day after bringing us a bag of groceries, Aunt Henrietta tried to comfort me with the old refrain, "No matter how bad it is someone always has it harder." Somehow it didn't make me feel better to know that someone was out there suffering more than I, and I said as much to my aunt. But she went on to tell me about a woman she had recently met at the Greyhound bus station while waiting to pick up a friend.

Aunt Henrietta sat at the coffee shop counter when someone tapped her on the shoulder. "May I kindly have fifty cents to buy coffee and some toast?" she asked in Spanish.

"I turned to see a short, heavyset, most unattractive woman before me. Her face was scarred badly, and she appeared to have lost most of her teeth," related Aunt Henrietta.

The woman, who introduced herself as Uva (which means grape in Spanish), explained that she had come by bus to the United States after some American tourists contracted her in Mexico asking her to be a housekeeper and nanny. They had even provided her with a one-way ticket to their home city. When she arrived and called her would-be employers, however, they told her they had changed their minds and wouldn't need her after all. As a consequence, Uva had been begging for food and sleeping in the ladies room of the bus station for over a month and had no idea what to do, since she didn't speak English and knew no one in that city.

I was appalled and asked Aunt Henrietta what had finally happened to Uva, and she replied that as far as she knew Uva was still living at the bus station. I felt an immediate need to find this woman and asked my aunt to take me to the station right away to see if she was still there. When we arrived, I saw Uva and immediately ran to her, hugged her, and told her she was coming home with me. Uva gratefully accepted and was both elated and relieved.

Aunt Henrietta worried that now I had another mouth to feed, but I told her that so far God had provided and would now provide for Uva too. Truthfully, the only thing that I was concerned about at that time was bringing Uva home with me.

She proved to be a ray of sunshine. Uva was always happy and loved to sing and dance. The children loved her and she them. She was so grateful for those things most of us take for granted or don't even notice in life like clean air after a rainstorm or a bird's early morning song. She treated every chore, even scrubbing the toilets, with a smile. She would often dance with the broom and treat it as if it were the handsomest of partners. My children and I laughed at her silly antics and waited anxiously to see what she would do next.

One morning she said to me, "I have been gathering bottles all week and have enough of the deposit money for you to take the bus into town and get a job." I was startled by this declaration and objected, "But Uva I don't have any type of training and why would anybody hire me?" But she quickly replied, "Oh, you'll be hired because you're pretty. Now put on your best suit and let me fix your hair. When you get into town, get off in front of that huge drugstore (Walgreens). Turn around and follow that little side street behind the pharmacy. Soon you will see a 'Help Wanted' sign in a little shop, and that is where you will work."

Although surprised, I followed Uva's instructions precisely and sure enough found the sign in the window of a flower shop. I told the woman inside that I was there for the position. I was honest about my lack of experience, and she dismissed me right away. But before I left, a cheerful man with bright red hair stepped out of the back room and asked, "What have we here, Dixie?" Dixie told him she had interviewed me for the job but found me lacking and would not hire me.

"But I'm the manager, Dixie," he argued, "and I say she's hired." "But why?" asked Dixie. "Because she's pretty," replied my new employer.

My new job enabled us to move closer to town and into a nicer home. For a time all was improved until I came home one day and found Uva crying. "I have been told it's time to leave you," she cried. I asked, "Who said it's time?" But Uva would just shake her head and not answer the question.

I had saved a little out of each paycheck for Uva, who had refused payment for her babysitting and help during those months that she was with us. I offered the money to her, but she flatly refused it until I told her it was important to me that she take it.

The next day on our way to the Greyhound bus station to drop Uva off, she asked Aunt Henrietta to stop the car and drop her off a few blocks before the station. I got out of the car to give her a hug, and then Uva hurried around a building and into a back alley. She had been with me and my family for about six months, and I couldn't bear to let her go so I decided to follow closely behind. But when I turned into the same alley, I saw a quick flash of Uva's skirt and then nothing. I was faced with nothing, but the entirety of an empty alley, which although short, was nevertheless too far for anyone to just vanish from sight. Uva was nowhere to be found. I walked all the way to the bus station, but there was no sign of her. I even waited at the station, but she never showed up.

Uva would often say in Spanish, "Where I lived was a palace com-
pared to this old house, but I'd rather be here than in my palace because I get to share it with all of you whom I love so much." I had set
out to rescue a stranger in dire need and that stranger had instead
rescued me.

In retrospect, whenever those of us who knew Uva remembered
her, we all agreed that there was something very special and glowing
about her. She brightened a room simply by entering it, and we felt so
much love and happiness just by being in her presence. She had
uniqueness about her that was beyond special and mysterious. But
then again, angels always do.

My Miraculous Mission from God

---··◁∞▷··---

Sunni Welles
Arizona
Spiritual Medium
Author of *Glimpses of Heaven from the Angels Who Live There*
Radio Host—*Ask the Angels* on Blog Talk Radio
www.sunniwelles.com

I don't have a college degree of any kind. I do not have a degree in theology or counseling, nor am I a student of metaphysics. I am, and have been, an actor since childhood, then later a dancer and singer of jazz. Intermixed with, desperately at times, trying to make a living in show business, I have been a waitress, bartender, gift shop salesclerk, car salesperson, office supplies sales manager, and a representative salesperson for a line of jewelry, make-up, and health products. I have sold encyclopedias door to door. I have been a telemarketing manager for large companies and small. I have been a cosmetologist, a masseuse, and more—if you can imagine.

But besides the difficult times in my life, there have been good times too, especially the several years I was blessed to perform and sing solo at the Debbie Reynolds Hotel in Las Vegas. I worked with some truly talented performers at Debbie's hotel, and I really loved that period of my life. I loved my friends, especially Debbie, and I believe that we all became like extended family to each other, which added an extra dimension to my life as an entertainer. This heaven was not to last, however. Debbie was having insurmountable difficulties with the hotel, and we realized that our little family was going to be broken apart.

There were some who held on there, in the last days, who felt such sheer sadness that it was palpable. I cried most nights because, after almost three years, this most wonderful dream was coming to an end. I was going through unmistakable anxiety about the separation that was fast approaching.

One night I was alone at home in my bedroom. It was about eight o'clock. I was on my bed praying to God to please help Debbie with whatever she needed so that this little show business family would not have to be disbanded and that I would still have a place to feel at home and feel loved. I also prayed that if it was indeed in God's plan that all this would come to an end, I hoped he would allow me to continue to entertain and to sing or at the very least that he might provide a day job that would give me enough income to pay my bills. I did not make a lot of money, and everything that I did make went to keeping a roof over my head or for something necessary for my career in show business. These needs were not molehills to surmount but mountains of great challenge. I told God that if these things couldn't be worked out, I wished he would just please bring me home. I was exhausted from the struggle.

It was in that moment of prayer that I had the realization that I was being just too self-pitying, too self-involved, and too self-absorbed. I decided at that very moment to change my prayer and to have faith and trust in God for everything. I decided to honor his will as he surely knows at all times and in every moment what will be best for us, both in our earthly needs as well as in our spiritual growth. I continued to pray, but my prayer changed completely. With the absolute intent of my heart I prayed, "Father, never mind everything I have just said and have asked you for because if it is not your will, Lord God, then I don't want any of it. I'm so sorry for my prideful requests and self-centered ways. Please forgive me in my self-pity, and let your will be done in my life. Father, thy will be done, whatever that might be. Make me your servant, Father, and bring to me the work that you have given me to do, no matter what that might be."

I don't think I have ever been more serious. I put my whole heart, mind, and body into my prayer. And then a miracle happened! As I mentioned, I was sitting on my bed. I was directly across from the floor-to-ceiling mirrors on my closet doors. In the instant after I said my prayer, I looked up and saw twinkling lights in the mirror. They appeared to be off in the distance but were very quickly getting larger and moving closer. There were two very bright lights with many other lights twinkling around them. Suddenly the two brightest lights took shape before me.

My first reaction was one of fear. Many thoughts were flying fast and furiously in my mind as I was thinking at the same time, *Oh my God, what's happening? Is this some sort of UFO or alien phenomenon? What is going on?* I remember I tried to say out loud in what turned out to be only a whisper, "I rebuke thee, Satan. I bind you in the name of Jesus!" My fear was such that for seconds it seemed I couldn't breathe. I followed my rebuke with the beginning of the Lord's Prayer, but by that time I began to feel a sense of peace come over me. It was a sensation of calming that I could never begin to describe with mere and totally inadequate words.

My fear subsided completely as I observed the lights beginning to change into two of the most beautiful beings I have ever seen—the most complete and total beings of light. They were opaque, and yet I could see through them at times to the mirror behind. They were such an incredible whiteness of light that there were beams of light shooting from their bodies and all around them. Behind their heads it was as if there was a spotlight that backlit what appeared to be shining auburn and brownish tones to the color of their hair.

One had long hair to his shoulders and the other had a shorter, more cropped, close-to-the head style. I noticed no jewelry or accoutrements that would distract my eye from their gorgeous, illuminative faces. One had very visibly sparkling blue eyes. The other's eyes, soft and tender, were a deep sea-foam green. The beings wore beautiful robes that were perhaps like those a monk would wear—only these were bright white and free flowing. They seemed to billow softly in an unseen, unfelt wind. They had gold and silvery shining sort of rope belts about their waists. The belts hung loosely to their hips with tassels hanging down to one side. The tassels also flickered with light. I was aware of their feet for only brief seconds, and when I could see them clearly, I saw that the beings wore some sort of sandals which wrapped around their ankles. The sandals appeared to be leather although I cannot be sure because I saw them for such a short amount of time.

At other times the bottom part of their legs didn't show at all, and the beings seemed to be suspended in midair. Each had behind him (they were both male figures) a pair of beautifully large and feathery iridescent wings which I could see the tops of but were closed and seemed to be attached to their backs.

I was in a state of complete and total awe! As I watched these beings, I realized that I was hearing words in my head. But as I looked at the beings' mouths moving, I saw that the thought sounds and words I was hearing mismatched the mouth movements. For a moment it struck me as funny because what I was seeing looked like one of those old foreign films where the dubbing of English words didn't quite match the mouth movements. In this case, the beings' mouths were moving in advance of the sounds I was hearing. I think I must have smiled and maybe chuckled over this.

But even though by then I was feeling totally at ease, I was still awestruck by what I was seeing. The words each being spoke came to me in a hushed yet amplified way. The thoughts also came very fast to my understanding just as a cassette tape that is fast-forwarding yet you are still able to understand it. I understood all their words. They had perfect timing—one spoke when the other would pause. Everything they said to me was set apart from the other thoughts that were still racing in my head. Their voices were distinctive. Each had its own melodious tone, and I would have been able to tell them apart even if I had not been watching whose mouth was moving.

I sat on my bed unable to move, dumbstruck as I heard the following words from these most wonderful beings of light: "Do not be afraid, Sunni, for we are angels of God, and we were sent by God to bring you that which you have requested of our Lord. Your mission and service to the Creator will be forthcoming and will be prepared for you by the angels who will soon follow us and come to you. You may ask what you will of these holy servants, and they will answer you. The Holiest of Holies will always be with you, as well as a host of angels assigned by God for your protection." "We offer our service to you as well, Sunni, as you are being called to your mission, as we also are willing messengers and servants of our Lord. We give you lovingly our blessings in that which you have humbly volunteered and been chosen, and in His Holy Son's name—the Christ, and our Lord Jesus. We must now take our leave. Peace and love be with you."

As the last few sentences were spoken to me, I realized that the angels' lights were beginning to move backward. They faded slightly as they floated back into the mirror from where they had come. By the end of the last phrase, "Peace and love be with you," their bodies had faded completely and became the two brightest lights with smaller particles, sparkles, and flickers all around as when I had first noticed them coming out of my mirror. They drifted backwards as if being pulled by some unseen force. Needless to say, if people had walked into my room and seen the expression on my face, I don't know what they would have thought.

I just stared into the nothingness of the mirror for several minutes before I dared move. Now I was able to see only my own stunned reflection staring back. When I was finally able to move, I went to my bathroom, and as I looked in the mirror, I splashed cold water on my face. I knew I would never forget the vision of the angels as it was burned into my mind in every respect. I knelt down and cried over and over again, "God, thy will be done." With tears streaming down my face, I thanked and praised the Lord again and again for such an unbelievable and transforming gift!

During the first several weeks after the angels' visit, things were still not going well in my life. As always, as part of my daily prayer to God, I had asked for help with my own problems as well as those of my family and friends. It seemed to me that everyone I knew was in the same position as I or was very close to it. I had no prospects of a positive nature, and I was at my wits' end. I went to God again. I should tell you that I have my own way of talking to God. I talk to him as though he is sitting with me wherever I am at the time. I talk to him in the same way I am speaking to you now through my writing.

I was telling him I didn't understand why I couldn't find a day job that I'd be able to hold on to and why I was having so much trouble finding singing work because I knew my voice was a gift from him. Why was he not giving me the chance to use my gift as he had in the past? I said to God, "You know, Father, that I love singing as much as I love breathing. But if it is not in your plan for me to sing, then please just give me a good day job that I can feel productive in and I will do what you want. I want to do your will."

I continued to say that if he wanted me to let go of all my possessions, I would—most things of value were in hock at the pawn shop anyway and that if it was his will for me never to sing again or to use any of the other gifts he had given me, I would give those up as well. I asked him to please end my financial troubles and give me a job that was his will for me to do, so that I would again find joy in living on this earth. I said to God, "I submit completely to your will. What do *you* want me to do?"

Let me backtrack a moment and tell you that my true conversion to Christ came in 1973 through my then in-laws Betty and Joe O'Banion. In the midst of all our problems, they helped me understand that I should "let go and let God." I had been a believer from my childhood, but in name only. I had not actually given my life over to God on a day-to-day basis to let his word and his healing direct my life. I finally realized that there was only so much I could do alone and that if I wanted to be able to face obstacles and challenges, I would need a spiritual anchor. I use the term anchor because I believe that God is not a crutch as some may feel. I give credit to God at all times for helping me handle whatever is happening even though there have been times I was sure he couldn't have been there with me when I was going through what I thought was more than I could handle. And I told him so many times.

I went to church as much as I could for many years. I would study the Bible when I could, either alone with tapes or with groups of people. But I was not a handing-out-pamphlets, witnessing-to-strangers, and praising-the-Lord type of Christian. I was not comfortable with the charismatic Christian behavior of raising my hands to the Lord. Nor was I ever able to be taken over by the Holy Spirit and speak in tongues—no matter how many times I pleaded. I still, however, had an abiding faith through all things that befell me that "all things work together for good for those who love God." (Romans 8:28) And I knew I most certainly loved God. Sooner or later it would all be all right.

Back to the present . . . As the days went on, I kept trying to find work. Friends were making sure that I ate at least as well as my pets. They were giving me money for gas for my car though I hadn't been able to afford the smog certificate, registration, or auto insurance. I also prayed that I would not be caught by the police and lose my license or worse yet, have an accident of any type while I was out trying to find work. The saying "When it rains, it pours" has applied to me on more than one occasion. I continued to hang in there as I always had and kept thanking God for what I did have. And then it happened!

The date was October 20, 1994, and I was at home. Things hadn't changed much. It had been approximately two or three weeks since I'd prayed the "I wish you'd take me" prayer. I was lying in bed at 10 p.m., writing my thoughts in a journal. (I have done this for years as a way to express my feelings, to sort things out, to let go of anger, to ask questions that I have no answers for, and generally just to vent.)

As I started my third paragraph, I stopped to think. My hand was still on the paper, but I hadn't yet formulated what I wanted to write next. All of a sudden my hand began to move by itself, and I watched in wonder as it spelled out in capital letters "IMMORTAL MAN." The next thing I knew, my hand and arm crossed the paper and wrote "LaurahereandTomYoungertoo." The words were not separated. They were grouped together in one long, smooth sentence. There was no punctuation. I couldn't believe my eyes.

I began to pray out loud, "Lord God in Heaven, please let whatever is happening here be of you and from you. I pray this in your son's name." Then I remembered the words of the angels: "Your mission and service to the Creator will be forthcoming and will be prepared for you by the angels who will soon follow us and come to you." The handwriting continued: "We are the ones the angels of God told you

(Sunni) would bring you your mission."

Since I was a born-again Christian, I knew that a spiritual gift like this one could also come from evil forces. I enlisted the help of a pastor friend of mine to test these spirits. Together for a period of over two months, we rebuked them in Jesus' name and asked them questions from Scripture. Only after this testing did we become fully convinced that they were, indeed, angels of God. What also helped to convince us was that these angels themselves told me that each time I allow them to use my hand I must first test them as Scripture indicates (1 John 4:1-3). At last, fully satisfied and with the blessing of my pastor friend, I gave myself over to God, his son Jesus, and the Holy Spirit.

The gifts the Lord has blessed me with since that time back in 1994 now include automatic writing, clairaudience, discernment, and the ability to call in a specific spirit for a session. Over the years hundreds of the bereaved have been greatly comforted by communicating with their loved ones through my God-given gifts. I feel so fulfilled, blessed, and humbled by it all.

The Face of Jesus

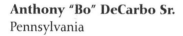

Anthony "Bo" DeCarbo Sr.
Pennsylvania

The day started out like any other. I lived a very hectic, active lifestyle in September 2000. In addition to my job as a full-time dispatcher with the Pennsylvania State Police, I was also a crematorium manager for my cousin's funeral home and kept busy volunteering at my church. There were never enough hours in the day.

But my life would soon come to an unexpected halt. When I was leaving my job as a dispatcher on September 25, a co-worker remarked, "I'll see you tonight." To this I replied, "If God wants us to." To this day, I don't know why I said this. But looking back, it is obvious that this was a premonition of sorts. The next day I woke up feeling as if I had acid reflux. Only it wasn't acid reflux, and surprisingly, I went on to suffer a major heart attack and was rushed by ambulance to the local hospital.

Doctors detected a heartbeat, but no brain stem activity which means there is no reaction to a stimulus. As a result, I was given less than a 1 percent chance of survival. I then needed to be transferred to a hospital that specialized in cardiac care. Several hospitals declined to take me because of the lack of brain stem activity, but I was eventually transferred to a hospital in Pittsburgh. Meanwhile a priest was called to give me my last rites. All the while my family and friends prayed feverishly for me, and a steady stream of visitors came to my bedside showing their support.

Through it all my wife Sandy refused to accept that I might not make it and continued to keep the faith. I was then taken to yet another hospital and another team of heart specialists. This time the doctor informed my wife that they had found brain stem activity. There was hope at this point, and my wife told everyone to keep praying for me.

Tests revealed that 99 percent of one of my secondary arteries was blocked. Doctors needed to insert a stent which works to open up the artery. I spent several days in the Intensive Care Unit (ICU). One morning, while still in ICU, I managed to get up out of bed, and I made my way over to the window. My room was on the eighth floor, and I happened to notice a helicopter lifting off in the distance. As I stood there curiously watching the helicopter, the face of a man suddenly appeared in the window.

Wearing a veil over his head and a beard, he had piercing dark eyes. Both astonished and shocked, I realized that I was looking at the face of Jesus. My whole body felt weak, and my heart began to race like crazy. I was wearing a heart monitor and knew someone would be coming in at any moment to check on me.

At this point, I looked at him and asked, "Are you here for me?" Jesus gave me a warm smile from the right side of his face and replied, "I am here for you but not in the way that you think. I'm here to let you know I am always with you." He then disappeared.

I sat back down on the bed, sweating with my heart still pounding. Mere words cannot describe both the amazement and the gratitude that I felt at that moment. I honestly didn't know what to think. Even though I knew it had happened, I kept questioning myself. I mean why would Jesus come to visit me? Who am I to deserve this?

Afterwards a priest came to see me, and I told him what had happened. He replied, "What makes you think that it didn't happen?" I realized then that I needed to trust what I knew in my heart. God was with me the whole time. His visit helped me to see firsthand the power of faith and prayer.

There are still times when I wonder, *Why me?* My only answer is that God has more work for me to do. I have no doubt that I'm still here because of him. Until we meet again, I will carry on and continue to do his will.

Time Warp

-----••◄∞►••-----

Claire Gardner
Virginia

As I looked through my windshield, the silhouettes played with my eyes. The moon was bright, and there were no street lights as I drove along the back roads to my job in Hemet, California. From my home in Moreno Valley I had two options: I could take the back roads and cut through farmers' fields which took forty-five minutes or I could take the freeway which would take me over an hour. On this day I opted for the more scenic route. I checked the clock noticing that it was 4:45 a.m. and figured I should arrive in just twenty minutes. In the meantime I was enjoying the early drive with no traffic in sight. For all intention purposes it looked like it was going to be a great day!

As I round the next curve, I see a barricade in the road and approach cautiously . . . DETOUR—DETOUR where?

I've driven this road to work for over a year now. There's a field, not a road unless they call this narrow dirt trail through the cow pasture a

road. I wonder how far this will take me out of my way. I try to pick up
speed in the sand and something darts in front of me; I brake and just
as quickly my car goes into a spin so fast that the scenery becomes just
a blur. I have no control of my car!!! My hands are on the wheel, but *I
am out of control!* Strangely, I feel calm. *What does this mean? I wonder, God,
if you're trying to get my attention. I'm listening.*

The next few seconds seem to happen in slow motion; the scenery
remains a blur as I continue the spin; suddenly there's a dull thud, a
collision, and I'm aware that I'm rolling over . . . slowly. My cell phone
sails past me, and I release one hand from the wheel to try to catch it.
I should call work and let them know I'll be late, I think to myself. *I'm in the
middle of nowhere, haven't seen a car since turning onto this dirt road. The car has
landed on the driver's side. I can't move . . . I'm still strapped in. I feel strange but in
no pain.* I'm trying to rationalize what just happened . . . *Where is that cell
phone?*

The only escape I can see is through the passenger door which now
serves as my roof. As I grope to free myself from the locked safety
strap across my chest, bright lights shine in front of me, and I flash my
lights for attention and say a quiet "Thank you, God." A stranger runs
over and asks, "Are you all right?" "I'm fine thanks," I answer. "I just
need help climbing out the passenger window and my cell . . . "

"I'll get help," he says and runs off! Great! Where is he going to find
help in this field; I just needed to get out of the seat belt. I struggle to
climb out; then I hear, "I got another guy." He's back?!! "We think we
can just roll you over; just hang onto the steering wheel and on the
count of three we'll lift the car." Is he kidding? With no time to think I
hear, "2—3—Heave," and then the roll, nearly turning over to the other
side but the car settles on all four tires! I'm still holding the steering
wheel and am dumbfounded. Before I can gather my thoughts, he
opens the car door and tells me to sit still so he can check for injuries.
"There's not a thing wrong with me," I say in total disbelief and get out
of the car to prove it to the three of us.

I ask their names and offer something for their wonderful assistance. Of course, they would not hear of it. "Where were you coming
from at this time of the morning?" Daniel asks. I tell him I was on my
way to work. They both smile, and Daniel says "You're headed in the
wrong direction." I describe the spinning, and he checks the road for

tracks. "Sure looks like someone spun a lot around here," he agrees. "You are one blessed lady. You came to a stop at the only sand pile around. Guess that's what knocked you over."

Gerry comes up and takes both of my hands in his. I'm taken back by the sincere look of concern showing in his eyes. He interrupts my stare. "I have a message for you from God." Embarrassed, I question, "You do?" He continues, "God wants you to slow down," he urges, "and to remember he is with you; keep him close in your heart." *What a sweet young man*, I think. "Thank you! I know I keep him and the angels mighty busy," I say awkwardly. Daniel then interrupts, "If you're going to work, we'll make sure you turn your car around alright; there's a nasty accident up ahead, and the cops aren't there yet. I trust they'll be putting up a road block soon so you'd better go before they do." I agree, and as I turn around, I roll the window down to smile and wave a final thank you . . . but I don't see them. I check my rear view mirror for truck lights, and it is dark. "WOW! They sure left in a hurry," I say to myself as I head down the road.

A few minutes later I turn off the detour trail onto the main road as I pass the accident and just down the road I see the police car approaching. Made it just in time, Daniel was right. *Wait a minute!* My senses seem to be returning as the reality of the situation set in. Daniel knew about the accident that I just passed. The rig should have been following me. Why did I never see the lights again? How did they know the police would not be there yet? Where, in fact, did they suddenly come from . . . and the message from God? Was that for real? No, no, no, of course not, my car and I are great; I have no pain whatsoever. Sometimes when I drive, I wander in thought a bit, and before I know it, I wonder how I got there. It is early in the morning; did I take a quick cat nap and have a major dream? WOW! That was surreal!

Dawn is breaking as I park my car. I pick up my cell phone from the floor, close the door, and check the driver's side as I lock it. It looks good. I'll just have to get a new side mirror and minor paint touch up, and it'll be good as new! I'm only seven minutes late for work; it's going to be a great day. I've been touched by angels in a rig.

My husband was a trucker, and he told me many times before he passed on, "If you're ever on the road by yourself and are in trouble, seek out a trucker. They're the angels of the road and always willing to help someone in distress." No doubt my angels were truckers in disguise.

My Lady in White

Edmund Rydell
Virgin Islands
Blog: www.spirithoughts.com
Author of *Eternity Revealed*

In the winter my wife and I reside in St. John in the US Virgin Islands. I had been to St. Thomas for some minor medical work and was on my way back to St. John. It was rather late in the afternoon because my doctor had asked me to wait until he had seen his other patients before performing this simple dermatological procedure. I was walking along the street that led to the main thoroughfare along which the open-air shuttle bus that went to the ferry dock would be running. It was past the rush hour; the street was deserted. There was no one on the sidewalks, and only an occasional car would come by.

Rather suddenly I became aware of a figure making her way toward me on the sidewalk, which, strangely enough, I had not noticed before. She was actually only a few yards from me. She was not young.

She was dark skinned and was wearing a long dress which completely covered her legs and feet. Her jacket was tightfitting with long sleeves. It had a row of little white cloth buttons up the front that led to a high collar. Her head was covered with some sort of headdress so that I was not aware of her hair. The whole costume was white or sort of a silver-white.

From the time I first noticed her, she was looking straight at me and continued holding me in eye contact as she approached. When she was almost abreast, she stopped walking and continued holding me in her smiling gaze. It would have been rude to walk right past her, so I stopped walking too.

I have often wished that I had memorized the exact words which she said. However, it was something to the effect of "I want you to know that what you are doing is the right course. You are on the right track." Somehow she seemed to be just radiating love and affection. Then she flashed a bright smile. I mumbled some sort of thank you, and she went on her way.

I also continued walking along. My first rationalization—*Batty old lady, dresses up at twilight and goes out and gives compliments to strangers*—was quickly replaced with a more rational thought. *You know, that was really strange*, I thought to myself. Everything about it was quite unusual. Suddenly I wheeled around. She was nowhere to be seen.

There was no place where she could have gone in that short amount of time. The buildings on the street were commercial, not retail and were closed for the day. Moreover, they were set well back from the street, too far to reach in the time that had passed. She hardly would have had time to cross the street, but there was nothing there she could have gone to. In short, she had simply disappeared. As I began to review the circumstances, it dawned on me what this really was—an angelic visitation.

First of all, her sudden appearance when I was under the impression that the street was deserted was unsettling, and her sudden disappearance was even more so. Her persistent eye contact as she approached was extremely unusual. Local people, black or white, simply do not do this. Her stopping just in front of me was unprecedented. And her initiating a conversation with a total stranger was something I have never encountered in many years of living on the islands, or for that matter, in our home on the mainland. People simply do not stop walking and start talking like that. And the costume! It was straight out of the century before last. It is almost inconceivable that anyone would be able to preserve such a costume in its pristine condition for such a long period. But the message she gave me was perhaps the most unusual of all. For her to be able to say what she did, she had to know quite a bit about me. I have no evidence that she wasn't referring to the way I comb my hair or brush my teeth, but I have to assume it was far more profound than that. I have to believe she was referring to what has become my life's work in recent years—writing about spiritual matters.

Before long I had to conclude that I had been visited by an otherworldly entity—one that conveyed a message which gave me renewed hope and strength for my endeavors. How I regret not having the presence of mind to recognize this when it was happening! How I would have loved to have found out more about her message and about her!

I have so often fantasized about what I could have said. "You're not from here, are you?" I could have asked. It would have been so gratifying to experience her no doubt ambiguous answer.

I still cannot think about this encounter at length nor write about it without experiencing a rush of emotion. It created an impression that has never left me, has not diminished in the slightest, and in fact, continues to be a high point of my life. Even though I have not seen her again, I like to think that my "Lady in White" still cares about me and is still with me.

My Two Light Beings

Barbara Harris Whitfield
Georgia
Author of several titles including: *Spiritual Awakenings: Insights of the Near Death Experience* and *The Natural Soul*
www.barbarawhitfield.com

I met Professor Kenneth Ring in the early 80s. I had written him after having read an article in *Omni Magazine* describing his research on near-death experiences at the University of Connecticut. I didn't tell him about mine in the first letter but did relay to him the ones my ER and ICU patients had told me about either as they were dying or when some of them had come back. They seemed to know I was safe or that I had had one too.

After several letters back and forth, Ken told me he was going to be speaking at a conference just a few minutes from my home in South Florida and invited me to come.

A few days before I met him at this conference, I went to the movies and saw *Resurrection*. I was totally overwhelmed by the story. Except for the cultural background, I was Ellen Burstyn's character.

After Ken gave his talk, he asked if anyone in the audience of about eighty people had had a near-death experience, and no one raised his hand. He asked if Barbara Harris was in the audience, and I sheepishly stood, shaking. And of course, he asked me if I could tell my experience. This was the first time I had told it other than trying to tell a psychiatrist seven years earlier (and then I was told I was depressed and handed a prescription for antidepressants that I never took.)

As I spoke, the words seemed to come from somewhere else, and I couldn't look at the people turned around staring at me. I kept gazing at Ken hoping that I wasn't embarrassing him and dreading the silence when I had finished. At the same time I was reliving my experience as it actually happened. And finally when I was finished, there was the silence I had dreaded—then there was a loud clapping noise and everyone was smiling at me.

The last thing I had talked about was having seen the film *Resurrection* a few nights earlier and relating how the character's energy helped others and how I felt "that" when I was working with dying people. Later, over a cup of coffee, Ken asked me to look up a word—a strange word I had barely heard before—and to write telling him what I thought. The word was "kundalini."

A few days later, a whole new world opened up for me when I stood in front of a book case in a store right across the street from my daughter's dorm at the University of Florida. One shelf was filled with books on kundalini. I bought three books: *Kundalini: Psychosis or Transcendence* by an American psychiatrist who had also been an ophthalmologist, another book by John White, and *Stalking the Wild Pendulum* by Itzhak Bentov. Bentov's book resonated with me the most. He talked about the physio-kundalini syndrome, and I knew that I had most of the signs and symptoms he described.

The letters started flying between Storrs, Connecticut and Pembroke Pines, Florida. Finally, not being able to contain my enthusiasm any longer, I wrote Ken and asked him if I could come up there to talk with him again. And he called to tell me that a letter from him was on its way (mailed the day earlier) inviting me up to the "near-death hotel" as his house was called in those days. It seems that many near-death experiencers had come to visit and tell him what they knew. And now he was writing his second book stemming from our interviews. We agreed that I would come up in a month and that's when the visits started. Late at night as I lay in bed thinking about all I was reading, two "beings" would float into the room from the doorway. (No, they did not come through any walls!) They barely had a shape that wavered and radiated a low pulsating light. So that I wouldn't become terrified over this, I told myself they were my grandmother (who had met me in the tunnel in my NDE) and my aunt whom I had adored. They stayed near the bed for several minutes, but I don't really know how long *because* when they were with me, it seemed as if time had stopped just as it had done during my NDE. This went on every night for the whole month.

The day I was leaving, as I was packing, I picked up a new book I had just bought by Itzhak Bentov called *A Cosmic Book on Creation*. As I tossed it into my suit case, I saw the back cover for the first time and jumped because there was Bentov's picture. He had died in the 70s in a plane crash. But that face was the same face I had seen over and over while meditating. He was trying to talk to me, but the "transmission" was garbled. This was when the worry about losing my mind caught up with me. Between the visits at night and meditating with a man trying to talk to me, I came face to face with my fear of this all being psychotic.

At that moment I made up my mind that I was going to tell Ken, who was a social psychologist, that I was seeing Bentov. If he told me I was crazy, I was going to turn around in the airport, get back on the next flight to Florida, and put all this behind me.

When I landed and Ken was standing there waiting for me, I stuttered and stammered, "Ken, Bentov has been trying to talk to me in meditation!" Ken's answer, rather dryly delivered was, "Bentov's been seen all over Boston!" (Boston was where Bentov lived and worked with many scientists while trying to prove his physio-kundalini hypothesis.)

Ken Ring's near-death hotel was an incredibly picturesque converted mill on a bubbling brook. It was New England at its finest and also my first visit to this area.

As I crawled into bed that first evening, there they were—my two beings of light who stayed just next to the bed until I fell asleep. And they were there all four nights. I looked forward to climbing under the covers and looking at them until I fell asleep because they gave me the kind of comfort I really needed. They settled down that voice in my head which kept asking me who I thought I was—this respiratory therapist who heard a few NDE and DE stories. Did that make me an important enough person to fly up to tell a professor what I thought I knew for a book about which I knew nothing?[3] My ego was relentless until I would look at my (now they were MY) two light beings and drift off to sleep. When I came home, they were gone. I knew they had served their purpose and needed to go on to someone else who needed their comfort.

Let's fast forward four years. I moved to Connecticut to become research assistant to Bruce Greyson, MD at the University of Connecticut Medical School. We looked at the aftereffects of NDEs including the kundalini hypothesis. We collected stats that were significant and published them showing that there really is an energy arousal after a "core" experience. That's what Ken had called deep experiences. So one evening I am lecturing at a hospice just outside of Hartford, and my audience was a group of hospice volunteers who were open and loving people. One of the questions thrown at me was about visitations from angels or other beings, and I opened up to tell them a lot of what I have just written above plus some amazing visitations that I have witnessed while sitting with someone who was transitioning. A cold shiver ran up my spine as I remembered that a reporter from the *Hartford Courant* was in the audience. *Oh my God!* I thought. *I am going to be the laughing stock of the medical school. And not just I but Dr. Greyson! It's going to be harder on him!!* I walked out of this meeting in a cold sweat.

I got in my car and started to drive the hour it took to get to my house. I looked in my rearview mirror on the verge of breaking down and crying, and there they were—in my back seat—my two light beings. I couldn't believe it, and I pulled over onto the shoulder of the highway and stopped. I turned around, and they weren't there. I started driving again, and when I checked my side view mirror, they

---

[3]Kenneth Ring's book *Heading toward Omega: In Search of the Meaning of the Near-Death Experience* came out two years later in 1984, and I was a key subject in that book.

were glowing from the back seat. I looked in the rear view mirror, and there they were. I started talking to them and laughing. Finally after telling them all my worries about bringing some kind of shame to my boss and me, I calmed down and told them I was feeling better. And within a few seconds after that, they were gone. I smiled for the rest of the ride telling myself we are never ever alone!

And by the way, the article in the *Hartford Courant* (and other affiliated newspapers across the country) came out a few days later, and my talk at the hospice was never mentioned. And it was a great article!

People Who Eat Tapioca

————••⟨∞⟩••————

Mary Ellen "Angel Scribe"
Oregon
Author, *Expect Miracles* and *A Christmas Filled with Miracles*, and award-winning photojournalist/pet columnist
www.AngelScribe.com
www.pettipsntales.com

A cancer diagnosis messes with your head, especially in the middle of the night. After I was diagnosed with breast cancer, I would lie awake, constantly worrying about the future. The surgery was successful, the healing had begun, but my spirit was still panicking.

One night as I lay down to sleep with the ever-present puzzling question about what direction to take for my health, I said a prayer to the angels, asking for their guidance.

The plain and simple truth was that I wanted to live. So I asked them for answers in the form of a clear dream—not one of those wild and cryptic ones that leaves you questioning your sanity in the morning.

What followed next was more than amazing. It literally was the answer to a prayer in the form of a dream or vision. Here's what happened:

The scene opened up in a blood-work lab. There were a number of technicians at lab tables—many of whom were very heavily depressed, as well as people of all ages and conditions of health walking around. A technician inserted a needle with very thin tubing into the top part of my arm above the wrist and instructed me to walk around until the thin tubing was full of blood. As I did this, I looked at the people around me; every detail about them would be recognizable if I saw them on the street the next day. It was as if this dream was talking to my soul.

There were drops of blood on the floors, on the techs' gloves, aprons. The dream was obviously meant to focus on blood. I was to pay attention to this information.

When it was my turn to have the blood work tested, I approached the technician, and he spotted a drop of blood on the immaculate white lab table from the person before me. He said the most intriguing thing . . . as if in slow motion, "Let me wipe up this drop of........ACID."

It was as if he definitely was saying that acid blood causes illness. After he wiped it up, he turned to me and said, "Did you know people who eat tapioca never have a trace of cancer in their bloodstream?"

I had no idea until the next day when I woke up and called an herbalist friend who said that tapioca is from the root of a plant in South America known for its medicinal properties. The friend said it alkalizes the blood. I have been eating it since and LOVING it. We make it with soya milk and no sugar and it is as close in flavor to the nectar of the gods.

In the dream the technician also said, "The trouble is you sit in front of your computer as if you are a monk cloistered in a cave. You need to walk three to four miles a day."

Well, that message was very clear! Get up and move the fluids in my body.

Then the dream ended. My panic abated, and a new life began. The angels had indeed brought me the desired clear information and direction to rebuild my strength and health.

The following week I asked for another dream message. Again my request was granted. During the night I had a dream where a pretty, young angelic–looking woman with shoulder length, brown hair came and stood before me. She told me, "You know some people can see into others' bodies and energy fields. I can, and you have no trace of cancer anywhere in your body; you must BELIEVE this."

At this writing it is over twelve years later, and I remain healthy. Now that I've shared my experience, I think it's time for a nice warm bowl of tapioca pudding![4]

---

[4]*DISCLAIMER: This information is for reference purposes only and not intended to diagnose, treat, cure, or prevent any health condition. It is not intended to substitute advice given by a physician, pharmacist, or other licensed healthcare professional. Always consult your physician.*

He Looked Just like Daniel

Orlando Bartolomeo
Pennsylvania
oreobartj@yahoo.com

My wife and I left our daughter's house in Ellport, Pennsylvania and were headed to a Trader Horn store. As we were traveling out of Ellport, we noticed walking on the side of the road a boy who looked just like our deceased son Daniel. Despite my shock I continued to drive past this boy, but my wife frantically pleaded with me to go back saying, "That's our baby! We have to go back!"

Daniel Bartolomeo

I immediately slowed down to get a better look at him, and the hairs on my back stood up. Not only did he look like my son, but he also looked at me the same way my son used to. We continued on our

51

way to the Trader Horn store still in shock over the incident.
Suddenly a driver speeding carelessly down the road went through
a red light, missing us by a mere few seconds. Looking back I realized
that had I not slowed down to get a better look at that boy on the
road, my wife and I would have been hit head-on by that speeding
driver. This boy, who looked just like our son, saved our lives. I have
no doubt it was our son, now Angel Daniel, looking after us.

The Hitchhiker

Kat
Mississippi
mississippi-mom@ymail.com

I was sitting in church listening to what I thought would be a typical Sunday sermon. Little did I know this one would actually turn out to be something extraordinary. Speaking on the topic of how it is important for all of us to place our trust in God, the pastor used a hitchhiker as an example. Hitchhiking, also known as thumbing up for a ride, became a popular means of transportation during the Great Depression when people sought help getting to various locations to seek work.

Nowadays, although we still do see an occasional hitchhiker, many are reluctant to help due to the dangers involved. So on this day in church, the pastor went on about how we let our fears overcome us when we see a hitchhiker instead of putting our trust in God. Because we don't trust enough, we pass him by, never giving him a second thought. Instead of assuming that this person is out to do us harm, he told the congregation that they need only pray to God for protection and give it a try.

A few days later with my best friend Hannah, I was driving into town heading north on Highway 27 in Monticello, Mississippi. Being on the road reminded me about the pastor's sermon so I filled her in on what he had told us as we drove. Then, lo and behold, we saw a hitchhiker on the side of the road. He was a young man with a large duffle bag holding out his thumb hoping for a ride. My friend is extremely cautious, and she was the one driving so she just passed him by. My conscience was really nibbling at me, and she knew it. I could just hear the pastor saying, "We don't trust God enough." After talking about the situation for no more than a minute, we made a hasty decision to turn back.

I knew my friend was hoping that someone had already picked him up, but he was still there. He climbed into the backseat and asked if we would take him as far as we could. He said it didn't matter how far it was. We were about three or four miles away from town, and although I wanted to ask my friend to take him further, I couldn't. I didn't want to ask her to use more gas for a stranger knowing that she struggled with what little she had. And I certainly didn't have a dime to offer. So I told the young man that we would drop him off at one of the stores in town, and he seemed extremely grateful.

As we continued to drive, we struck up a conversation, and he asked me if I knew a particular woman. I was taken back because I did indeed know this woman. Ironically, she was in fact one of my fellow parishioners at church. Soon we reached the store and he offered us money, but we refused it.

The following Sunday I saw his sister at church and walked right up to telling her that I had met her brother. She gazed at me with this confused look on her face and said, "I don't know what you are talking about!" I was completely stunned and told her that the hitchhiker had told us that she was his sister. She assured me, however, that she had never head of this man and that he was not her brother.

Well, I thought, isn't that strange? But then again, the Bible does tell us that we never know when we will come face to face with an angel. Many times these angels are here to teach us a lesson. For me, that lesson was to learn how to trust in God a little more. I learned that having faith is not about believing that God can protect us. Faith, instead, is about believing that he will. We need only trust.

Protected in Roswell, New Mexico

Demetria
North Carolina

My family is from Roswell, New Mexico. Roswell, as most people know, is well known for the UFO incident that occurred in July 1947 when debris resembling an alien spacecraft was found. Allegedly, alien occupants were also found, and the city has been the subject of controversy and various theories ever since.

Although I can't give credence to any of the UFO hyperbole, I can tell you about an unforgettable incident that happened to me in the late 70s. Back in 1978 my sister was in the air force, visiting us on leave. My father had bought property in a neighboring town and was busy remodeling the house on the property so that we could all move in. We had been there most of the day and were on the road in the outskirts of Roswell in a left turn lane waiting for traffic to clear. I was lying in the backseat sleeping while my stepmother drove and my sister sat in the passenger seat. Keep in mind that this was way before seatbelts were mandatory, and none of us had been wearing one at the time.

I was beginning to come out of my sleep when I suddenly felt and heard us being hit by another vehicle from behind. The other driver hit us hard at sixty miles per hour, sending the trunk lid flying off the car and pushing the rest of the trunk into the backseat. Somehow, through all the loud screeching and window shattering that was taking place, I found myself lying on the floor in between the front and back seats. Had I been sitting up, I likely would have been decapitated.

The tremendous force of the accident pushed our heavy, big 1977 Ford LTD into oncoming traffic. My sister and stepmother just braced themselves for the worst, not knowing what else to do. But what is unusual about this accident is that just before the impact, the outside of the car went dark for a few seconds. In other words, we could see inside the car but couldn't see what was taking place outside the car. Although we couldn't temporarily see what was happening, we could still hear the screeching sound of the other vehicles on the road, trying to avoid hitting us. There we were in the midst of oncoming traffic, yet no one at all hit us.

When the car finally came to a complete stop and the darkness lifted, there was glass in every direction for at least fifty feet. Every single window had been shattered, and the gas tank had ruptured pouring petroleum all over the road. It all seemed to happen so quickly, and I can't remember how we managed to eventually get out of the car, but we scrambled out and made our way to the side of the road. The car was, in fact, still running, and my sister had to go back to turn off the engine.

The police officer investigating the accident was extremely amazed. He just couldn't figure out how we had gone into oncoming traffic without being hit. It made no sense to him how we were even alive given the condition of our car which was now completely mangled with most of the trunk in the backseat. The officer also told us that the skid marks left from our vehicle started out straight, then disappeared, and then started up again in a 180-degree like angle which resembled a "T." He had absolutely no explanation.

Looking back, I don't have an explanation for what happened either. It was as if an angel or God decided to spare us and just lifted us out of harm's way. Again this was a huge, heavy car. How is it possible for the skid marks to suddenly stop and then start up again? What happened in between? And incidentally that time in between is when the outside of the car went dark. So I can only assume that we were not meant to see what was actually taking place.

The guy who hit us tried to leave the scene of the accident, but he admitted that his girlfriend made him stop. He was not paying attention, leaning down to fix something on his radio, when he looked up to see us and slammed on his brakes.

Roswell may be most famous for the alleged extraterrestrial activity which took place in 1947, but to me and my family Roswell is famous for a very different type of otherworldly experience. It is the place where an angel lifted us out of harm's way.

My Divine Guide

Stephanie Pope
Virginia
smpope@cox.net

When I was twelve years old, my family planned a summer vacation to Lima, Peru to visit my aunt and uncle whom I had never been able to visit up to this time. I was terribly excited because I had never flown on a plane before and we were going to take a side trip to Machu Picchu—a place that I had read much about in my beloved archaeology books. Finally the day came when we boarded a train near Cusco and lumbered slowly through the mountain passes to this magnificent peak. We spent the afternoon with a tour guide, learning about the terraces and the daily life of the Incas, but around 4 p.m. we had to return to our hotel onsite because the mists descended around the peaks, wrapping the area up for the evening. A real sense of mystery and wonder filled my heart, and I couldn't wait for the coming day to explore the area more.

The next morning dawned bright and sunny. As luck would have it, I got to shower first, and while my parents and brother were dressing, I wandered out of the hotel where I saw a stone path that led one over the next hill and on to other unknown adventures. I was drawn to that path as if it were magnetic. Since the mists of the previous night had lifted, I felt compelled to walk that trail. As I started to climb the hill, a priest in a long robe appeared to my right. He, too, seemed to be looking at the pathway. I greeted him in my newly acquired Spanish vocabulary whereupon he smiled at me and pointed back toward the hotel. Being the obedient girl that I was, I stopped walking on the path and headed back to the hotel. I turned to see if he were following me and much to my surprise I could not see him anywhere. Thinking nothing of it then, I returned to the hotel for another day of sightseeing.

I didn't tell my parents about this story, and it has been only recently that I have recalled this encounter. Now that I am older and reflecting on the special moments in my life, this episode fills me with awe and respect for God and reinforces the idea that we are never truly alone. I am grateful that such a guide would appear in a form that I would respect and follow. Who knows what might have happened if I had continued on that mountain path alone!

---

[5]**Author's Note:** Machu Picchu, located in the Cusco Region of Peru, South America, was built by the Incas around 1450. It sits on a mountain above the Urubamba Valley. Many archaeologists believe that this incredible cultural site was erected as an estate for Pachacuti, the Inca emperor from 1438–1472. Restoration work for this popular tourist attraction continues today.

A Knowing Beyond Knowing

Pete Boraks
California

As they say, things happen for a reason. When I was twenty-one, my college girlfriend dumped me for an older, more successful man. Although I was devastated back then, I realize now that it was this very experience which started me on my path toward spiritual awareness. And for this incident I will forever be grateful. I am a longtime member of the Edgar Cayce's A.R.E. (Association for Research and Enlightenment). Each day I strive to live my life according to Cayce's recommendations and readings.

For those of you who may not know of Edgar Cayce, he was recognized as America's greatest psychic and performed thousands of readings during his lifetime. While in a self-induced trance state, he was able to answer questions on everything from the beginning of existence to spirituality and health. In fact, he was a medical clairvoyant who was able to offer cures to hundreds of people. He founded the

A.R.E., a nonprofit organization, in 1931, and his timeless readings continue to help thousands.

Let's fast forward a bit to 2001. At this time I was living in Switzerland and working for Nestlé Corporation on the shores of Lake Geneva. I was walking home alone late one night after a few too many drinks. Losing my balance, I fell down a small hill and hit my head on a stone wall. I lay on the ground for some time, unconscious and bleeding. Looking back, I'm certain that I would have died had it not been for a divine intervention.

Someone woke me up and told me that it wasn't my time yet and to get up. I say someone because I don't quite know how to describe this entity. I remember feeling that it was a female presence but yet not a woman. I know that doesn't make sense. But perhaps the best way to describe it is to say that it was both male and female, yet of no particular sex.

Somehow I managed to stand up and began to groggily walk along until a Good Samaritan found me and called for help. I was taken to the hospital by ambulance and surprisingly survived the whole ordeal with just a few scars. I know things would have been much worse had it not been for the angel who woke me up and told me to keep going.

Again let's fast forward now to a day in 2010 just before I did my daily meditations. I was reading about how we need to go inside ourselves to find Jesus. A bit later as I began to meditate, I decided to ask Jesus some specific questions. I asked, for example, if my grandmother was near me during a recent psychic reading with a medium. I asked this because it had troubled me that the medium had seen only my grandfather and not my grandmother.

I continued to meditate and eventually reached a very deep trance-like state. Suddenly I felt the presence of the Blessed Mother. There was not a doubt in my mind that she was there with me. I could feel her presence. In fact, I could sense her just to the right of my head. It is difficult to describe with mere words, but I can only say that I felt an overwhelming sense of happiness and joy. The feeling was very strong and a huge smile grew both on my face and in my heart. I was just completely elated.

Afterwards I wondered why the Blessed Mother had come to me, and then it hit me. My grandmother had always had a strong devotion to Mary. She was devoutly Catholic and always carried the rosaries around with her. She would pray to the Blessed Mother all day long. Admittedly she had a special relationship with Mary that I had never quite understood, but on that day I did finally understand. The Blessed Mother came to let me know that my grandmother was there with me. I know to some people this may seem crazy or irrational. Believe me when I say that I can certainly understand. Before retiring I was a highly successful auditor who based everything on facts and numbers. Even now I have to see hard evidence before I believe anything.

And yet when I was blessed with my divine encounter on that beautiful day, I can only say that I got all the hard evidence I needed. It was a knowing beyond knowing.

Angels in New York State

---··◄∞►··---

Mary Ellen Szwejkowski
New York
tjjjjm@gmail.com

Back in the summer of 1995, we were in the midst of shopping around for possible colleges in New York State for my oldest son. We live on Long Island, which is about thirty miles from New York City, and my son wanted to visit SUNY (the State University of New York) in Plattsburgh. SUNY is situated in a small town amid roughly 256 beautiful acres. It is just twenty miles away from the Canadian border and about fifty miles away from Montreal.

The college is a five-hour drive from our home, and we had never been to that area before. The day we decided to make the trip was a bit rainy as I trekked along in unknown territory. We had left at 5 a.m. and it was now about three hours later when I realized that I was almost out of gas. I was driving on the New York State Thruway as my son slept soundly in the back seat.

Trying not to panic, I got off the nearest exit hoping to find a gas station, but instead I found myself in a heavily wooded, isolated area. There was no gas station in sight. My anxiety was rising and my heart pounding as I looked at the gas gage and saw that it was now past the empty mark. And to make things even worse, it was a foggy morning; I got lost and couldn't even find my way back to the entrance of the thruway.

Imagine my surprise when I suddenly saw a pickup truck with two men inside pop up seemingly out of nowhere. Desperate for help, I began waving them down, knowing this wasn't the safest thing to do. Thankfully they stopped, and I asked the truck driver for directions to the nearest gas station. They both wore caps on their heads and were clean shaven. One had on a plaid shirt while the other wore a plain solid blue shirt. They were both very kind and told me that the nearest station was five miles away and proceeded to give me directions.

Although I was very grateful for their help, I told them that my car was out of gas and that I wouldn't make it there. What happened next took me by surprise. Even though I pleaded with them telling them that I had no gas and even asked if they had some gas they could put in my tank, they insisted that I would make it. I also asked them to please look at my gas gage, but they confidently refused. One of them even remarked, "I know you're empty" and kept insisting that I go to the gas station.

The whole time that this was happening, my son was still sleeping peacefully in the back seat. Even though I was puzzled and certainly didn't believe that I would make it, I had no choice but to try. I thanked them both, and as I was leaving to head to the gas station, I took one last glance in the rear view mirror. To my shock and disbelief, there was no one there. They had completely vanished.

As you might have guessed by now, I did make my way to the station without running out of gas, much to my relief. At the time I wondered, *How can they be so sure I'll make it?* But today I can only say that angels have a way of knowing everything.

Let George Do It

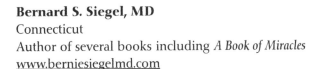

Bernard S. Siegel, MD
Connecticut
Author of several books including *A Book of Miracles*
www.berniesiegelmd.com

Many years ago I attended a weekend workshop run by Dr. Carl Simonton to learn more about how to help care for and empower cancer patients. When he announced that he was going to lead everyone in a guided imagery session, I thought he was wasting my time. I sat with my eyes open, watching him as he led everyone through the exercise. When he looked down at me, I thought, *He will know I am not doing it if I have my eyes open.* So I closed my eyes and became a believer.

I am an artist and very visual. When my eyes closed, I was amazed at the visions which presented themselves. When Carl said we will now meet our inner guide on the path we were walking, I thought, *Well, I'm a doctor so Jesus, Moses, or some equally important figure will appear.* The man coming towards me was dressed in a white robe and sandals, had a full head of hair, a beard, and a unique cap on his head. When he came up to me, he said, "My name is George." That was quite a letdown for me. However, as I spoke with him that day and in the following years, he has always been filled with wisdom and was very aware of my feelings and needs— both spiritual and practical. He was just as likely to tell me when I needed new clothes as to tell me how to deal with my life, my family, and my patients' needs.

At a workshop I attended, I drew a picture of George, my imagery scene, and path for Elisabeth Kübler-Ross. I also included other symbols and guides such as a bird named Rainbow and a fish leaping out of the water. I talked to all of them during my meditations. I was amazed at how much Elisabeth knew about my life from this random drawing. I drew twelve trees, and she asked why twelve was important to me. I had been doing this work twelve months. She asked, "What are you covering up?" She explained I had used a white crayon to draw snow on a mountain, but the page was already white. So the added layer suggested I was covering up something. She was so right related to me burying my feelings and emotions as a doctor.

I also realized that the rainbow was a symbol for me to get my life and emotions in order as each color represented an emotion. The fish out of water represented me and my life at the time.

What else has been mystical for me? I have had four experiences in my life where I could have died or been seriously injured. As a four-year-old I was choking to death on a toy I aspirated. I left my body, had a near-death experience, and was quite angry about not dying. For a four-year-old, being out of the body was far more interesting than being in it. Twice my car has been totaled, and in one accident I was thrown from the car, before seat belts, and yet each time I walked away with no serious injuries. The last event was when the top rung of my ladder snapped off as I was climbing down from the roof of my house. I landed on my feet on the pavement, toppled, and banged my head, but again no serious injury.

I really had a sense that someone took me and put me safely down because there was no way to explain how I could land past the ladder on my feet. When I shared this with a group, one man said you do have an angel and I know his name.

I asked, "What is it?"

He replied, "What did you say when the ladder broke?"

"Oh, shit."

"That's his name."

I think his name is George, but I have now given him a nickname. Since then I have had some more accidents that I will not go into detail about, but I think calling his name always makes a difference in my walking away free of serious injury.

The most mystical part of my experience with a spirit guide comes not from what I feel, but from what other people have seen and reported to me. One night I was giving a lecture and having a difficult time following my outline and notes. I began to feel the other talk which was coming out of me was better so I just let it happen. When the lecture concluded, a woman came up to me and said, "That was better than usual." I agreed with her, and the next woman who came up said, "Standing in front of you for the entire lecture was a man and I drew his picture." There was George with his full head of hair and beard. It was an incredible moment for me.

Several years later I delivered a Sunday sermon at a friend's funeral. After the service I was standing alone in the hallway when healer Olga Worrall came over and asked, "Are you Jewish?"

"Why do you ask?" I said. I thought she was relating to a question about my giving a Sunday sermon.

"Because," she answered, "there are two rabbis standing next to you." She went on to describe them, and they were exactly the same description I would have given of George. I learned from photographs I found later that the unusually shaped cap he wore was a Yarmulke or prayer cap that was common a century ago.

Since those events I just let George do it. I literally never prepare in any detailed manner for my presentations. I bring things with me which I may use or refer to, but I just let it happen. I always feel that between George and the audience communicating with me the right things will be said.

I know from my life experience that consciousness is non-local and can exist without the body. I have had communications from the dead—individually and through mystics. I have learned how to communicate with animals and to listen to the voice, or George, which speaks to me and tells me to ask things or do things and always had significant meaning in my life.

Here are three simple examples. I wrote a book called *Buddy's Candle* to help people cope with the loss of a loved one. When it was finished and I was walking my dog Furphy, a voice said to me, "Go to the animal shelter." I got into the car and went to the shelter. When I walked in, there was a dog sitting by the door.

"What's his name?" The voice asked speaking through me.

"His name is Buddy. He has been here less than fifteen minutes."

"I am here to take him home." I did and now we have two dogs, Furphy and Buddy.

I was out jogging, before going to the hospital to be with my dad when he died, when a voice asked me, "How did your parents meet?"

"I don't know."

"Then ask your mother when you get to the hospital."

When I arrived at my dad's bedside, the first words out of my mouth were, "Mom, how did you two meet?" The stories began with the words, "Your dad lost a coin toss and had to take me out." The stories that followed allowed my dad to die laughing and made the day an incredible experience.

One other time that the voice, or George, helped me was in caring for a dying teenager who asked me, "Why am I different?" He was asking me why he was dying when other kids his age were out in the street playing. The voice answered, "Because it makes you beautiful." I was about to apologize for the statement because I thought it was cruel, but when I looked at Toni's face, he was beaming. Again the voice, or George, saved me.

Since then, I have heard from my deceased parents and many others. So I know their consciousness continues to exist, and for me George is the spirit guide who helps me stay focused and on my path through life. How I know this is that he used a dying friend I was visiting at hospice, who, when I entered his room, looked up and said, "Hello, Journey." We had been friends for years, and until that day he had called me Bernie. So my journey continues until George and I will become one by joining together in the great collective consciousness. And if you ever get into trouble or an accident, you know who to call when you need guidance and help.

My Escort Angels

Donna Wolfe Gatti
West Virginia
Author, *Angels and Alchemy*
www.angelacademy.com
donna@angelacademy.com

My first encounter with what are known as escort angels occurred in 1974 during a life-changing near-death experience (NDE). While undergoing a surgical procedure, the doctor made a mistake, cut an artery, and I lost too much blood to sustain life. As my physical body lay dying on the operating table, I rose up and surveyed the situation. I noticed that the doctors and nurses were upset and were working desperately to save me. In my now ethereal body with my mental faculties and personality still intact, I went nose to nose with each one telling them to relax, that I was okay, but they just ignored me. Frustrated, I moved higher up, away from my body, and began to fly. Gravity had no effect on me. Flying was natural and effortless, sort of like swimming underwater, but in an ocean of brilliant white light.

I heard a kind and gentle Voice speak. Without my asking, the Voice answered all the big questions about life. Then my smallest concerns were addressed as if they were matters of great importance. When the Voice told me why Aunt Bettie married Uncle Fred, I giggled with joy and contentment. My curiosity had been completely satisfied, and I felt like a child held in the arms of a loving parent after a hard day at school. The Voice in the light had anticipated and joyfully fulfilled my needs and desires with good humor, extreme love, and enormous tenderness.

Suddenly I was interrupted as the nurse yelled, "We're losing her," and at the sound of distress I was propelled upward. The farther up I went, the brighter the light became. Two cherubs appeared, one on either side of me, and we slowly drifted to the corner of the ceiling. We communicated through mental telepathy, which is faster and more efficient than mere words. They told me they were escort angels and had come to take me home. But before we could go, I had to look at the body I was leaving behind. She was only twenty-five years old and in perfect health, except for the loss of blood and spirit. I determined that the situation was not serious enough, and in less than an instant I re-entered my physical body through the navel. I was back on earth and suffering from homesickness.

I looked up at the ceiling to see the escort angels fly through the wall, and I became emotionally distraught. I was embarrassed because I had forgotten to thank them for coming to get me. Years later, whenever I thought about my lack of good manners, I cringed inside. One day I heard one of them say, "Why don't you thank us now?" I laughed, relieved that I could right a wrong. I then said, "Thank you," and saw balloons, confetti, and two tiny cherubs dancing in celebration.

Since my NDE, I have had many other mystical experiences and constantly seem to walk the bridge between heaven and earth. The angels have chosen me to deliver their messages. I don't hold a college or professional degree of any kind, but then again I don't need one. My credentials are simply my very profound and mystical experiences, and my teachers are simply the angels themselves.

An Angel in Shoprite

Jill
New Jersey

My wonderful maternal grandfather's name was Saverio, but everyone who knew and loved him affectionately called him Ace. As he
grew older and approached his mid-80s, he began to have trouble
getting around and accomplishing his chores. So whenever he needed
to go anywhere or do his weekly grocery shopping, either my mother
or I would take him to the local Shoprite. I cherished these trips because they gave me a chance to spend one-on-one time with him.

After he passed, I had trouble going to Shoprite. Although I had
happy memories of all our food excursions, I was not ready to let him
go. Going there made me so emotional and not seeing him was just
too painful for me, so I avoided the store like the plague for a while.

When I finally worked up enough nerve to step foot in the store
again, I was filled with all the feelings I had expected and was having
a hard time controlling myself. I stood there temporarily motionless

struggling to hold back tears in one of the aisles I had so often fre-
quented with my grandfather. Suddenly, I developed this terrible itch-
ing cough. I looked up and down the aisle feeling embarrassed but
thankfully saw no one.

Unexpectedly an older man with grey hair wearing tan clothing
walked around the end of aisle towards me with no cart and no bas-
ket. As I looked at him, he reminded me of my grandfather who also
wore tan colored clothing more often than not. I was shocked when
he then stopped directly in front of me and said, "Is that you coughing, little girl?" I'm sure my mouth must have hit the floor because
that was exactly what my grandfather always called me. I was his
"little girl."

I stood there, still stunned by this turn of events, knowing that
there was no reason for this stranger to call me, a grown woman, "little
girl." I then replied that it was indeed I who was coughing, and he said,
"Put out your hand." Even though I thought this was an odd request
from a stranger, I did as I was told, and he then placed two wrapped
cough drops in my hand. They were the same brand and type of cough
drops my grandfather always carried with him!

Just when I thought things couldn't get any weirder, the man looked
at me and said, "I am an usher at church, and I always carry these in
my pocket in case someone needs one." I was now completely speechless, feeling as if I was going to faint. My grandfather was a devout
Catholic and served as a weekly usher for his church. And he, too,
always carried the very same cough drops in his pocket for the same
reason . . . just in case someone needed one.

The man then patted me on the back and said, "Take care of yourself, little girl." I was still standing there, both speechless and motionless as he then quickly disappeared around the aisle. At this point I
could no longer control my emotions, and quite honestly I didn't care
what people thought. Tears began to pour down my face as I realized
that something beyond special had just taken place.

I also realized that I had never even thanked this stranger and now
wanted to tell him what a gift he had just given me. So I ran down the
aisle in the same direction this man had just left about thirty seconds
before and began searching for him. With no luck, I walked up and
down the aisles like a crazy person looking for him. He was nowhere

to be found. Where could he have gone in such a short span of time?

Now desperate, I decided to wait by the exit doors hoping to catch him on his way out, but he never showed up. At the time I can remember feeling disappointed because I so wanted to see this man again. But looking back, I realize how foolish this was of me. Angels don't need to use doors. They can come and go as they please.

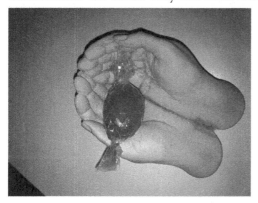

After my experience, I placed one of the cough drops at my grandfather's grave. The other one remains wrapped and secure in a drawer as a constant reminder that angels are real. And what's more, my grandfather always was and always will be with me.

Above is the cough drop that I kept, sitting in the figurine called "God's Hands."

When Cars Fly

Mary Joan Breit
Kansas
joan.breit@gmail.com

Angels have surrounded me all my life. There was never any doubt or question in my mind as to their existence. I have my mother to thank for that as she was the one who first introduced me to the Guardian Angel Prayer as a child and later made me fully aware of the nine choirs of angels. The Guardian Angel Prayer was an integral part of my evening prayers. For those of you who may not have heard of this prayer, it goes like this:

> *Angel of God, my guardian dear,*
> *To whom God's love commits me here,*
> *Ever this day, be at my side,*
> *To light and guard, rule and guide. Amen.*

A true believer in the power and grace of the angels, my mother explained that angels are actually part of one of nine choirs or orders. These heavenly choirs (Seraphim, Cherubim, Thrones, Dominions, Powers, Authorities, Principalities, Archangels, and Angels) represent various levels of angels who watch over God's creation and do God's will.

Gratefully I have had various angelic encounters throughout my life. Looking back, I often wonder why I have been gifted with such experiences. My only response is that perhaps it's because I grew up with a minimal sense of defined boundaries and had complete trust in the presence of angels. Because of this I have always been very intuitive and sensitive to both the environment and the people that I have encountered. And I've always understood that there is more to life than meets the eye.

When I reflect on all of my experiences, however, one stands out among the rest and will forever remain vivid in my mind as though it happened just yesterday. I was driving home after visiting with my sister who was undergoing intense ovarian cancer therapy. That day while I sat with my sister in the hospital, I read to her from the book *Where Angels Walk* by Joan Wester Anderson. The book, which I had just purchased that day, contained various accounts of angelic interventions.

I was impressed by many of the amazing accounts but skeptically remarked to my sister that although these divine events were great, nothing this extraordinary had ever happened in my life. Later, after leaving the hospital, I stopped to visit my Uncle Jerry and let him know how my sister was doing. When our visit had ended and I finally began the eight-hour trek home, the major interstate highways were ice free, but the less-traveled roads were ice covered and glistened like crystal lakes.

By this time the sun had disappeared over the horizon, and I decided to take a well-known shortcut down a gravel road, hoping to get home sooner. I had grown up nearby and was very familiar with the area. As I began the eight-mile trip to the next black top highway, I began to regret my decision and wished I had remained on the interstate. The further I traveled on the dirt road, the more treacherous the ice became. I crept along slowly at about ten to fifteen mph. Because of the stress, my body was stretched as tight as a fiddle string; farms were few and far between, and I saw no welcoming farm lights. I felt completely alone and desperate.

To make matters even worse, my car was almost out of gas. Rather than fill up earlier, I had chosen instead to fill up at the next upcoming town, not knowing what was in store for me. So there I was with my car running on empty. I had no warm blankets or any other emergency supplies should my car slide into the threatening graded ditches. Should I be stranded for the night, I knew I would certainly freeze to death.

Many morbid thoughts crossed my mind as I crawled along hopelessly with total dependence on Providence. Suddenly my worst fears became a reality as I felt the car sliding into a graded ditch. Panic stricken, I knew I could not put the car in reverse with any success because the car would be stuck diagonally.

BUT WAIT! Shockingly, I realized that my car was not sliding into the ditch but unbelievably going over the ditch. Yes, it was in the air and somehow flying over the ditch into the field. The motor had died, and I just sat there in disbelief, taking deep breaths feeling as if I was in some sort of science fiction movie. The car ended up landing in an unfenced, icy field in the same direction I had been driving. My mind was in a whirl as I contemplated what had just happened.

Still in shock, I started the car with the motor purring on the initial try and slowly made my way back to the entrance of the field several feet from where I had landed. I drove back onto gravel road and eventually back to the highway in a daze, not fully understanding what had just occurred. Although confused, my heart was overflowing with gratitude as I reached the next town and pulled into a gas station.

As I zoomed on home, I thought of the Guardian Angel Prayer and the nine choirs of angels. Earlier that day I had doubted that I could ever be blessed with an incredible angelic experience such as those mentioned in Joan Wester Anderson's book. But I think the angels decided to teach me, the skeptic, a lesson. I will never doubt again.

The Lady in the Light Gray Gown

William
Arizona

I can still see that gentle, sweet smile on her face—no judgment, no condemnation, just understanding. She understood everything and anything there was to know about me. My thoughts, my fears, my passions and secrets—she knew and understood everything the way no one else on earth ever could. Although it is difficult to describe my divine encounter with mere words, I will try to do justice to my unforgettable experience with the lady in the light gray gown.

For stress relief and relaxation, I would go up into the Arizona Mountains to ride my trail bike and take long walks in the forest. At this time in my life, I was very skeptical of religious beliefs and doubted consciousness survived physical death. Even though I considered myself an atheist/agnostic and I was pretty sure that God was in the same category as Santa Claus and the Easter Bunny, I started to pray on my hands and knees, asking to be shown the Other Side.

With a PhD in science, my beliefs were basically that this physical world was the only reality. But I suppose even though I was an atheist in my mind, my heart still hoped that I was wrong. I craved some sort of proof that there was more to my existence than the physical. Although I was grateful for my success in the corporate world, my life was missing something. Material things and money had done little to bring me the peace and happiness that I sought. So I felt I had no choice but to try to seek help from a higher source.

For several years I continued to travel to the mountains and pray. Then, finally, my answers came in 1990 over a two-week period in the most unlikely of places . . . my dreams. In fact, I had not one but three vivid dreams. The first two consisted of being shown beauty and nature beyond mere words. The forests were a beautiful vibrant green while the lakes were a brilliant bluish green. I floated effortlessly about 100 to 200 feet off the ground, witnessing the incredible beauty below. I later learned that what I had experienced are often called garden dreams during which we are shown the astral world or what some refer to as paradise in our sleep state.

The third dream was so profound that not a day goes by when I don't think about it. I remember every minute detail as though it had just happened even though more than two decades have passed since. A woman, who looked to be about forty-five years old with shoulder-length gray hair, wearing a light gray gown that paled in comparison to her hair, came to me. She stood about ten feet away from me as we looked intently into each other's eyes. I stood there mesmerized by her radiant smile as we engaged in telepathic communication. No words were spoken nor were they needed as she knew everything there was to know about me.

It was an instantaneous life review. She had perfect understanding of all my past and present feelings, emotions, and thoughts. She knew not only what I had done, but also why I had done it—even the most selfish acts that I will someday take to my grave. Absolutely nothing I had ever done was hidden from her, yet there was no judgment or condemnation, only total acceptance and love.

This entity then opened her arms as I effortlessly floated toward her. When our bodies touched, we both shared an unearthly vibration that was pure ecstasy. After this incredible spiritual hug, the dream or vision ended, but its effect will be with me forever. I could literally feel her entire energy field or aura as an incredible form of vibration.

I will never forget the total acceptance and love that I received from this most compassionate woman with the sweetest of smiles. As I said earlier, it was beyond any words or feelings I ever used or experienced on this earth. The best I can do is to say it was pure ecstasy that surpasses my ability to define my feeling or state of being.

Looking back, I believe this woman was a spirit guide who came to show me the true meaning of compassion and to fulfill my quest for answers. It reminds me of a popular verse from the Bible: "So I say to you, Ask, and it will be given to you; Search, and you will find; Knock and the door will be opened for you." Luke 11:9 (NRSV, Catholic Edition)

A Dream of St. Jude

Michael Occhibone
Pennsylvania

My brother had to have a liver transplant in 1993. Prior to going into the hospital for the surgery, he was living with my family and me. It was a long and painful process, and we weren't sure if he was even going to be able to have the transplant. He did, however, and sadly after fourteen hours of surgery, the liver began failing once again. As a result, he had to have a second transplant. It was hard enough getting the first one. Finding two livers in such a short period would be a miracle in itself. He did miraculously get a second liver, but unfortunately his body was rejecting this one as well.

At this point his doctor called me and told me that my brother's vital signs were very weak, and he wasn't confident that my brother could survive another surgery. The doctor wanted to know what my family and I wanted to do.

I replied that I realized weighing the option of giving my brother yet another liver or possibly losing him because he was just too weak was an important one, but I assured this doctor that my brother was strong and a fighter. We wanted him to live! As far as I was concerned, there was no other option. I asked him to please consider giving my brother a third liver transplant if one became available. That same night I had an incredible, vivid dream.

In my dream I was in a big courtyard. The courtyard was all brick, and there were many doors everywhere, all with a few steps each. At the end of the courtyard was the main entrance with wider steps. There I noticed about eleven men standing around looking at something and crying. I walked over to them, standing behind them trying to see what they were looking at. When I did, I saw that it was a three-dimensional picture of Jesus. The picture was one of only his head with a crown of thorns and blood coming down his face. They all suddenly disappeared.

One of the doors opened, and a man came down the steps and walked over to me. He looked like Jesus, except he had gray in his hair and wore a beard with a mustache. He asked me what was troubling me. In response I told him that my brother was very ill, and I was afraid that he was going to die. There were two big candles there, probably about four feet high, and he asked me to light one for his intentions and one for those of my family. I did as I was told and lit the candles. When I did, the flame shot up to the sky on both of them. At this point I woke up.

Shortly after I had this dream, my eldest sister Judy asked me if I wanted to go to a novena with her. I did and it was a St. Jude Novena. While there, I saw a picture of St. Jude and immediately realized that this was the man I had seen in my dream. I learned later that St. Jude was Jesus' cousin, and he is known both to have a flame on his head and also to carry an image of Jesus with him. He was also one of Jesus' apostles. This information thus explained why I had seen so many men in my dream. They were the apostles.

A couple of summers after I had had this dream, I was watching a television program which showed Pope John Paul II at a youth rally in Mexico. I was shocked when I noticed there were two four-foot candles next to him . . . the same candles that I had seen in my dream.

Another amazing thing that I need to mention here is that I noticed

The courtyard at the Vatican in Rome

a dome in the courtyard when I had my dream. I tried many times to figure out what the significance of this dome was but couldn't. I knew it had to mean something. The answer came in 1999 when my wife and I went to Italy to visit family and friends. While there, we went to the Vatican and saw the Sistine Chapel. It was beautiful. On our way out, we went down the steps into a gift shop. I walked down this walkway and turned to my left. When I did, I saw THE COURTYARD IN MY DREAMS! The dome that I had seen was that of the Vatican. The bricks are still there, but now there is grass in the courtyard with a modern sculpture in the middle. The doors are all blocked now and the steps are gone, but you can tell that they were once there.

Words cannot express how flabbergasted and stunned I was. When I saw it, I knew immediately that this was the place I had seen in my dream. When I returned home from Italy, I happened to watch something about the relics of saints on television. That's when it hit me. I did a Google search on the computer to find out where St. Jude's body was buried. And sure enough, St. Jude is entombed at the Vatican!

Author's Note: Michael's brother passed away on November 18, 2011 after having lived with the third transplanted liver for eighteen years. Before his death he had prayed over the phone from the Intensive

Care Unit with his niece who was diagnosed with uterine cancer, which
spread throughout her body into her lymph nodes. Afterwards doctors performed a hysterectomy on his niece. At that time, however, no
trace of cancer was found.

It's Me, Mom

Artie Hoffman
New Jersey
artiehoffman.com
artieonthemove@comcast

Everywhere I went, people seemed to bring up Lake George in upstate New York. As a psychic medium I knew that this was not a coincidence and that someone was trying to tell me something. Then one day I got a call from a woman requesting an appointment for a reading. The day was September 23, 2010, and we had unusually warm, beautiful weather on the East Coast. So before we hung up, I casually asked her what she had planned for the wonderful weekend we were expected to have. Her response, "I'm going to Lake George for a balloon festival."

I liked the idea of going to a balloon festival in Lake George as I hadn't been there since I was a kid, and the balloon festival sounded like a lot of fun. Plus my weekends are usually booked with psychic parties, and I happened to be free that weekend (a rarity). Thinking that this was a sign, I decided to make the trip and asked my friend Dawn if she wanted to go with me. She loved the idea, and we agreed to leave very early Saturday morning, around 6 a.m., to make the nearly four-hour drive up.

We were heading up Route 87 North on the New York State Thruway when I began to notice the number 24. I saw the number on three separate license plates and was convinced that this meant something. I happened to have my angel numerology book with me in the car and looked up the meaning of number 24. According to the book, this number has special significance and indicates that extra angels are surrounding you and will be with you throughout the day.

A few minutes later, Dawn looked toward her right and noticed the most beautiful ray of sunshine beaming through the clouds. It was absolutely breathtaking, and she wanted me to take note of it saying, "Artie! Look how beautiful that looks!" At this point we were both in awe of the view, and Dawn grabbed her camera to capture the moment on film. In response I told her that she was going to capture angels in the picture. My words were surprising even to me but as a psychic medium I've gotten used to these psychic or intuitive outbursts.

Sure enough, there were angels in the pictures. In the picture on page 93, for example, you can see Archangel Michael and even his sword below. Plus notice the brightness of that one section in the sky. Dawn and I were awestruck by what we had captured on film but as they say, the best was yet to come.

After taking the pictures, Dawn reminded me that this day was the anniversary of her daughter Brittany's death. Her daughter was only five months old when she had died of complications from Down's syndrome. "Do you think this is a message from Brittany since I asked her to give me a sign?" she wondered. We were feeling very overwhelmed by both the message of the number 24 and then the angel pictures.

As we continued down the highway, I suddenly remembered a reading I had done for Dawn a few months prior in which I had told her that her daughter was present. I shared with her that her daughter was going to give her a message to let her know that she was around.

The photo of Archangel Michael taken that day. Notice the sword to the left of the date stamp.

She would do this, I continued, by way of a butterfly.

When we finally arrived, we found that the balloons couldn't launch due to poor weather conditions; it was too windy. Nonetheless, we parked my car and began to scope the grounds, visiting various vendor booths. The first thing we saw was a man flying a kite in the shape of a butterfly. We both smiled acknowledging the sign from Brittany and continued to walk around doing some casual shopping.

Later we opted to go to a place called "The Village" which we were told was very scenic and right on Lake George. We enjoyed the ride and took some more pictures. On the way I happened to notice an OTB (Off Track Betting). This is a place where people can make all kinds of bets on various horse races. They have many different races going on at the same time from different states live via TV screens.

Again that intuitive voice kicked in, and I asked Dawn if she wanted to stop at the OTB. I told her, "There's going to be a horse with a name that is connected to your daughter. I'm telling you it's going to win!" I'm not sure if Dawn really believed me or if she just wanted to appease me, but we went in and we browsed through all the different races and programs that were going on.

After a short while, Dawn walked over to me and asked, "Do you think this might be the horse we are looking for?" I stared at the name of the horse with such excitement I could hardly control myself. The name of the horse was *It's Me, Mom*. I looked at Dawn and said, "**ARE YOU KIDDING ME?!!!!** You can't get much clearer than that! That's the horse. That horse is going to win!"

We continued to also search for other names and other races. We found another one named *Angels from Heaven* and decided to bet on that one too. Again we kept looking and found a horse named *Hot Air*. We thought that was interesting since we had come here for a balloon festival and you need hot air to launch a balloon. So you guessed it, we bet on this horse as well.

We walked up to the betting counter excitedly and told the guy that *It's Me, Mom* was definitely going to win the race. In response he told us that this particular race was not scheduled to start until 8:30 p.m. that evening, and they were about to close early that afternoon at 1:00 p.m. The guy assured us, however, that there was another OTB in the next town that was open until 11:00 p.m. Well, there was no way we were going to miss this race. It was a sure thing!

So we left the OTB to get a bite to eat and then made our way to The Village where we listened to live music and had a great day before heading back to the balloon festival. Weather conditions were still not favorable for the balloons to launch, but there were tons of people standing around. There was hardly a place to stand without being trampled on. But we were there and decided to make the best of it, finding a spot to relax on the grass and enjoy the moment. Just a few minutes later, a family with Down's syndrome children sat down just a few yards from us laughing and having a good time. Dawn recognized this as yet another sign from her daughter and remarked, "Look at that! This is a sign from Brittany. She is letting me know how happy she is in heaven."

Dawn and I hung out for about an hour just listening to the music and really enjoying the whole experience until it was time to head over to the other OTB. When we arrived, we shared our story with the girl behind the counter telling her that we were sure *It's Me, Mom* was going to win. We bet on three separate horses and three different races.

Angel in Heaven raced earlier but did not win. It came in seventh place. The second horse, *Hot Air*, did not race so I got back my $20 bet. At this point we wondered could this have been yet another sign. The balloons never did go up that day, and *Hot Air*, the horse, never ran.

We still had another twenty minutes before *It's Me, Mom* was scheduled to race, and Dawn went out to smoke a cigarette. At this point I began to pace back and forth, feeling that the horse was going to win by at least three or four lengths. There was just no doubt in my mind. When it was finally show time, *It's Me, Mom* was the number 10 horse, and there were twelve horses in the race. The bell sounded excitedly, and *It's Me, Mom* was one of the first horses out of the gate. The race was a short one; they had to go only halfway around the track. Number 10 took the lead as the other horses were following behind it. Suddenly the horse pulled further and further into first place. Halfway into the race, *It's Me, Mom* was already winning by about five lengths. Then came the final turn into the home stretch, and the horse was winning by a commanding lead to end the race.

It's Me, Mom won that race by ten lengths! I won $73.00 that glorious day, and Dawn won $60.00. People always ask me if I regret not betting more money on the race. Truthfully I have to respond both yes and no. Yes, because I certainly could have used the money. No, because everything happened according to divine plan. Both Brittany and the angels knew exactly what they were doing.

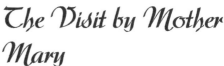

The Visit by Mother Mary

Franklin Castro
Colorado
Alfranktc@aol.com

I was living in downtown Denver directly across from a beautiful cathedral known as the Cathedral Basilica of the Immaculate Conception. The church is one of the oldest sites in the city and has beautiful gray stone on the outside while the inside is ornate with breathtaking stain-glassed windows. I was living in a small apartment nearby unemployed, lonely, and extremely depressed.

Since childhood I have always had a deep respect for the saints and the holy Mother Mary and her son Jesus. I began to immerse myself into the mystic traditions of the Catholic faith and started to say the rosary twice a day, once in the morning and again in the evening at the cathedral with the rosary group. I soon found myself at peace and no longer felt depressed.

As the prayers continued, my life began to improve slowly, my heart softened, and the events in my life that I thought were out of sync began to change. My mood lifted, promising job leads began to materialize, and I had renewed faith and trust that everything would be alright. One morning after visiting with my rosary group, I entered into my apartment and was taken back because I could clearly smell the scent of roses. While the scent was strong and beautiful, the air in the room also had a peaceful and loving energy about it that is difficult to describe.

I did not do anything to produce this fragrance, such as use candles or incense. It was so unexpected and stunning that I searched all over my apartment, looking for the source of this beautiful smell. Although I could not find the reason behind this scent, the smell continued and actually lasted for several more days. Visitors to my apartment even commented on how beautiful they felt the smell was so I knew then and I know now that it was not a product of my vivid imagination.

At first I thought that it might have been an angel that came but now feel that it was a heavenly visit by Mother Mary. There have been many Catholic accounts which document that when the apparition of Mary appeared, she left the smell of roses. It is said to be her trademark.

Regardless of whether it was an angel or the Blessed Mother Mary, I am so deeply blessed to have been honored with such a divine visit. Thinking back, I can only say that I experienced the holy of holies.

No One Ever Died Alone

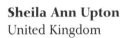

Sheila Ann Upton
United Kingdom

In November 2011 my father-in-law became ill and was admitted to Heartlands Hospital in Birmingham, UK. One night my husband and I went to visit him, and he asked us to draw our chairs closer to his bed because he had something important that he wanted to tell us. The tale that followed was a welcomed surprise.

He explained that two men had passed away in his hospital ward that day. In one case he saw two angels appear. The man's daughter had been sitting at her father's bedside and drifted off to sleep. As soon as her head fell forward in sleep, two angels appeared above the bed out of nowhere. They both floated down, and one went to each side of this man, supporting his wrists and elbows as they gently lifted his spirit, floated back up, and disappeared.

Soon after, the nurse walked into the ward to check on the man. When this nurse found that he had no pulse, she woke up his daughter to let her know that her father had just passed.

Naturally in shock, this woman walked over to my father-in-law and said, "He's gone." To this my father-in-law Albert said, "I know, my dear. You have his body, but I can promise you that his soul has been taken."

I was totally astonished by this because I know my father-in-law would never say such a thing if he hadn't really seen it. When I asked him what the angels looked like, he told me that they were two female angels wearing long white gowns and that they both had blond, curly hair. He also noted that they had small wings behind their shoulders. For some reason, he could not see their faces. When I asked why he thought their faces were concealed from him, he replied, "They had come to do their duty, and that's what they did."

Soon after, another male patient in the ward was getting ready to crossover. My father-in-law again witnessed visitors who came to take the man's soul to the Other Side. Only this time they did not look like your typical angels. Albert told us that two very tall, smartly dressed men appeared in black, wearing old-fashioned long coats and hats. Unlike the angels, they did not walk into the ward but rather just appeared. They walked close to my father-in-law's bed all the while looking at the man. Finally, they said that they would be back later, turned around, and walked through the wall.

This man passed on shortly after. It is important to note that this took place in a small hospital ward or room with all but four beds so my father-in-law was close to everyone else in the room and had a close-up view of both the angels and the men dressed in black. I've often wondered why the souls of these two men were taken differently and have even discussed it with Albert, but we both have no idea why.

Albert is very sensitive to the spirit world and has had spiritual experiences in the past. But this one is quite special to me because it lets us all know that the soul does indeed continue on. Although I felt sad for the families of these two men, it was so comforting to hear that both of them were not alone. Speaking of his experience, my father-in-law said, "No one ever dies alone, good or bad. There is always spirit there for him."

God Has His Way

---·•·❮∞❯·•·---

Hannie
Singapore

One day when I was little, we were having a party. Family and friends were coming in and out of my house. Suddenly out of the blue, three men came walking in a single row, dressed all in white, wearing white turbans and kaftans. They headed straight to our bedroom where I would always say my prayers. I asked my companions if they saw the three men, but they only gave me a strange look which I at first just shrugged off. Unsatisfied, however, I decided to go to the room and see if they were there but found no one.

Later I asked my mother who these three men were. She only smiled and told me that they could have been my guardian angels. My mother then related to me that when she was giving birth to me, she had a difficult delivery and was in severe pain. Three men looking like "wise men" appeared to comfort her and help her bear the pain. These three men, she said, stood by her side, encouraging her through the delivery. Although I realize how amazing this is today, at that time I just bushed it off as nothing.

Years later I had eaten something extremely spicy. This was nothing out of the ordinary since I love spicy food and would often indulge in these fiery chilies. But what I went through on this particular day really puzzled me. My stomach burned so much that I had turned as white as white paper and was sweating profusely. I literally thought my stomach would burst and I would die; that's how bad it was.

Not knowing what else to do, I drank a glass of milk, knowing that this was the best remedy for the burning. I then went up to my room to try to sleep it off. The air conditioner was on and was blowing air straight through a plastic bag which I had beside my bed. The bag began to ruffle and make noise so I reached for it thinking that the contents of the bag would spill out. Just as I did this, I clearly felt someone caress my side.

It is truly very difficult to describe how real this was. There was no one there that I could see yet I could clearly feel someone caressing me. I jumped from the shock of it and ran downstairs. When I did, I suddenly realized that the pain was gone. I was still afraid but at the same time very thankful to whomever it was that had taken my pain away.

Thinking back to what happened, I realize that I never even said thank you to the invisible visitor who caressed my side and took my pain away. I sincerely regret that, but I'm sure whoever it was knows of my gratitude. God has his way of sending angels to help us here on earth.

Angel Wings

George Thorp
New Jersey

Twelve years ago I experienced what I thought was nothing at the time. Eight years later I experienced it again and understood that it was no coincidence. In 1998 I was driving to work on a rainy day when I became distracted. When I regained my focus, I realized I was too close to stopped traffic in front of me. I slammed on the brakes, fishtailed, and struck the right rear of the car directly in front of me.

This caused my car to spin and strike two more cars in the center and far right lanes. My car continued to careen onto the side of the road, missing a road sign, and eventually striking a tree right behind my driver's side door. I walked out without a scratch although my car and the two others were destroyed. During the entire episode a warm safe feeling enveloped me. I gained a sense of calm, and it felt as if someone were telling me it was okay and nothing would harm me. I vividly remember the chaotic sequence of the accident, but never did

I feel fear. Afterwards I thought maybe this was a reaction of the brain to the extreme stress of the situation. I didn't think much about it until eight years later.

I needed to fix the covering on my furnace pipe located on the roof. Again it was a rainy day, but this time it was New Year's Eve. I needed to fix the pipe because I was concerned that water would drip down into the furnace. As I put my ladder against the side of the house, I was worried that I would slip and fall off the roof. I never got the chance to get on the top of the house, however, because the ladder slid out from beneath me as I stepped on the last rung before the roof.

As I fell to the ground, the same warm feeling came over me again. However, this time, I sensed what felt like two hands grabbing my shoulders. I landed straight on my feet perfectly as if someone had gently lowered me down. I did sustain a deep gash to my hand from the gutter, but it could have been much worse. Nowadays I no longer think the warm feeling and safe outcome in the above related experiences were coincidences or reactions to stressful situations. There are no coincidences.

The wings of an angel have protected me twice so far and I know always will. I thank God for every day I'm alive and try to give back by trying to make the world a better place with my actions.

The Three $1 Bills

Cindy Bigham
South Carolina
csutton1959@gmail.com

In 1964 when I was five years old and my sister was four, we were staying with my dad while my mom was at work. I walked into the living room to find my sister sitting on the floor with a bottle of aspirin, eating them. I thought, *Hmm that looks interesting, I want to try some.* We sat there and ate about sixty or more between the two of us.

Although my sister consumed more than I did, it was a large dose for both of us. I was sitting there feeling really dizzy, and suddenly I heard a very calm female voice say, "Drink a lot of water." I had no idea where this voice came from, but I did as I was told. I got up and filled a gallon glass pickle jar with water. I gave it to my sister who drank nearly the whole gallon, and then I drank. For some reason, my mother, who was at work, had a horrible feeling come over her. She later told me that she couldn't shake this feeling that something was wrong and that she needed to come home.

Leaving work immediately, she entered the house finding my sister and me in a semi-unconscious state. My dad was asleep in the bedroom and hadn't even realized what was going on. My mom gathered us up, and we were rushed to the hospital. The doctors pumped our stomachs, but by this time my sister was in a coma, strapped down with her eyes taped shut.

We were put in beds side by side but separated by a glass wall. My sister was near death, and I was touch and go as I drifted in and out of consciousness. My body ached badly, and I was overcome by fever. At some point I woke up and saw a beautiful woman standing at the foot of my bed smiling at me. She was dressed in a beautiful long, flowing white dress. I remember looking from her to my mother, wondering why my mom was not acknowledging her or talking to her.

Every time I would look at the woman, who seemed to be invisible to everyone else, I could feel total love and compassion. She did not speak with words but telepathically told me that I was going to be okay and not to worry about my sister. She would be alright as well. She then smiled a beautiful, warm smile, put her hand over her heart, and pointed above toward the heavens. It was all so real, and I will never forget it.

After four days in the hospital, they released me. Then on the fifth day, my sister came out of her coma. She was perfectly fine and got to go home just a few days after me. About ten years ago my sister and I were discussing things that had happened to us when we were little and we started talking about the aspirin incident. My sister remarked, "Yeah, I remember that. Who was that woman in white standing at the foot of the bed?" Taken back, I asked her how she could have seen this woman since she was in a coma at the time with her eyes taped shut. Not surprisingly, she couldn't explain it and neither could I. We called my mom and asked her who the woman was, and she said that she, my dad, and the doctors were the only ones allowed in the room. There was no woman with a white dress, at least that she could see. My mother's statements only confirmed what we already knew . . . this was an angel reassuring us that everything was going to be okay.

Lucky for me, this was not the only time I had the privilege of being visited by an angel. My son Michael VanGieson passed away on Feb 9,

2002. Immediately after his death, I began to receive messages from him. In fact, one of my afterlife communication experiences is in Josie Varga's book *Visits from Heaven*. About a month or two after my son's death, I was so depressed and mad at the world that I felt as if I was ready to end it all!

I was sitting in my husband's truck one night, listening to music, crying, and asking God, "Why? I hate you! How could you do this to me?" I just couldn't believe that God would do this to me and asked, "If there is a God, prove it to me." I also added a few choice curse words to that comment.

It was late at night. My husband and I couldn't sleep. So we ended up in the truck, listening to music and hoping the refreshing night air would help ease the pain of losing our son. Suddenly, there was a knock on the window on my side of the truck. Completely startled, I looked up to see a very handsome black gentleman smiling at me. I rolled down the window without any fear, and he said, "I ran out of gas down the street, and I was wondering if you have some gas or maybe a few bucks."

Usually I would be afraid of being approached by total strangers, especially late at night, but I told him to hold on a minute and I would look to see what I had. I had no gas to give him, but I did have three $1 bills. I offered the money to him, and he accepted it gratefully. My husband then offered him a beer, and the next thing I knew the three of us were out on my porch talking.

As we were chatting, I couldn't help but notice that this guy was smiling the entire time. There was something very comforting about him, and I found myself telling him about my son and how sad I was. He just stood there listening patiently as I vented, and although he didn't say much, he had a very calming demeanor. I also couldn't help but notice that there was a glow about him.

After some time he got up to leave saying that he needed to get back to his car and thanked me for the gas money. Then as he was walking away, he turned around one last time and said, "God bless you!" Less than a minute later, I grabbed my husband's arm and said, "Come on, let's give him a ride to his car." As we were getting in the truck, the man disappeared into thin air. We were in shock and tried to figure out some rationale for what had just happened. Where did he go?

We decided to go for a ride to try to find the man's car. We rode up and down every road near our home, looking for a disabled vehicle on the side of the road that looked as if it was out of gas but found absolutely nothing. When we returned home, we still couldn't sleep and stayed up until the wee hours of the morning, talking about our incredible encounter. The whole thing brought us both to tears as we knew something extraordinary had taken place.

Eventually I went to bed, and the next morning I woke up, still thinking about the night before. As I got up, I could hardly believe my eyes. There on the night stand were three $1 bills—the same ones that I had given to the mysterious man the night before. I knew then and I know now, without any doubt whatsoever, that this was an angel. I had asked for proof that there is a God and I had gotten it.

Two Very Tall Ladies

Lottie
Pennsylvania
lottiewoodcity7@yahoo.com

In 1985 my husband Charles decided to take a walk and never re-turned home again. Nothing bad happened to him. He had simply decided that he was through with our marriage. I waited, hoping to hear from him, but after two weeks I was beginning to give up hope, knowing that he would not return.

Then after two months, I decided to go to Pittsburgh, Pennsylvania to see if I could find him. Why did I go to Pittsburgh of all places? I had prayed and asked God to show me where he was, and God did just that. A little voice inside me told me to go to a church in Pitts-burgh and that is where I would find him. I decided to trust that voice.

I will never forget the day; it was a sunny Sunday afternoon in August of 1985 as I made my way to the church. My mind was so full of questions. Why did Charles leave? What was wrong with our marriage? Why did he leave without saying anything? I had so many questions yet no clue what was even wrong. I wasn't asking to revamp my marriage; truthfully I wanted only answers. Yes, admittedly I was still very upset, but I didn't want to cause a scene. All I wanted was for my husband to talk to me.

As I arrived at the church, the most unusual thing happened. Two very tall ladies met me at the main entrance and asked me if I was Lottie, Charles' wife? To my surprise, I said yes and thought to myself: *Who are these people and how do they know about me?* It all happened so fast. There I was wondering who these ladies were, and then, before I could say anything, they told me that I was going to be the speaker for the afternoon services. What? I didn't know these ladies, and they didn't know me. Why would they ask me to speak?

I couldn't help myself and started laughing in response. I said, "No" and could not stop laughing. Honestly, I thought it was the funniest thing I had ever heard. I had never even spoken before a large audience before. But one thing led to another, and all I can say is that I felt as though the Lord was telling me that I could do it.

Unbelievably I did speak before the congregation that day. I read from the Bible Corinthians 13: 1–7 (KJV) which is about the gift of love:

If I speak in the tongues of mortals and of angels, but do not have love, I am a noisy gong or a clanging cymbal. And if I have prophetic powers, and understand all mysteries and all knowledge, and I have all faith, so as to remove mountains, but do not have love, I am nothing. If I give away all my possessions, and if I hand over my body so that I may boast, but do not have love, I gain nothing.

Love is patient; love is kind; love is not envious or boastful or arrogant or rude. It does not insist on its own way; it is not irritable or resentful; it does not rejoice in wrongdoing, but rejoices in the truth. It bears all things, believes all things, hopes all things, and endures all things.

Looking back, I can only say that I was used by the Lord that day. After the service was over, Charles came over to me and we talked. Although I was really mad at first, I calmed down and was able to turn a bad situation into a good one. We later divorced, but because of my experience, I was at peace with it.

Your Son Will Be Safe

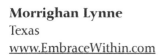

Morrighan Lynne
Texas
www.EmbraceWithin.com

Despite popular belief, working with angels hasn't always been my forte. And to be completely honest, at one point in my life I wasn't even open to working with anyone, let alone divine beings of light. Life experience had shown me that if I was to survive in the world, I would have to do it by myself. Slowly but surely and at a very early age, I had accepted the belief that no one could be trusted and everyone eventually hurts you.

So when I noticed angels were trying to communicate with me and requesting that I let go and trust them, you can imagine my resistance. Plus my understanding of angels was that they were of a certain theology and at that point in my life I really wasn't up for having religious experiences.

I had done the "church thing" when I was a kid. And although I had found solace and support in a community when I didn't find in my own family, I was past that point in my life. I had walked away years ago, setting out to discover the path that worked for me. So when angels came knocking at my door, my resistance was apparent. I wanted nothing to do with them, their messages, or their support. And yet it didn't deter them from trying to get through to me.

Part of me was afraid that the only reason they were there was what I had done wrong in my life, and the other part was just plain stubbornness! So I just kept pushing them away and continuously resisting their offerings. But then, things suddenly changed, and I couldn't ignore them any longer.

Living in Arizona at the time, I had just become a new mother. My son was the most amazing thing I had ever done in my life, and when I looked into his eyes, for once I saw the potential to be more than I had ever thought possible. He was about two months old when I got word from back home that a really good friend of mine had been killed in a car accident. He was the coolest kid in school, and during Texas summers we enjoyed building the occasional fort or tree house together. But what was even more tragic was how the letter noted how his mother was on twenty-four-hour suicide watch because of the grief of her loss.

This moved me to such a degree that I was paralyzed with fear. I was sitting on my sofa, nursing my infant son and thinking to myself that I would have to prepare for that possibility one day. The thoughts raced through my mind as I put myself in her place. Being no stranger to loss and sadness, I knew the world was full of disappointment and chaos. But being a mother made the stakes that much higher.

As I sat, holding my son and trying to wrap my head around how I was going to get ready for something like that, I felt a beautiful, warm hug wrap my back and arms from behind. And I heard the softest female voice say, "You do not to have to worry about that; your son will be safe."

I felt a deep comfort in her words and began to cry from the gratitude that I felt. It was, in an instant, everything that I wanted to hear, and yet I knew it meant that I wasn't going to be able to ignore these beings any longer. With this pivotal message also came awareness, and being in denial just wasn't going to cut it anymore.

This was the moment my life changed in more ways than one. My road with the angels hasn't always been easy, but I've learned over time that as long as I'm open to their messages, they have always led me in the direction that best supports my life. My preconceived notions about them were completely wrong. They have no interest in telling me how I'm living my life, only to offer other perspectives that I may not be aware of. So with baby steps and a few falls, I am happy to put my life into their hands and will continue to make every decision with the help of their counsel. But I think what has been the greatest impact for me is the knowing that I'm not in this alone—that I do truly have trustworthy friends who are in my corner.

In the Eyes of an Angel

---••⟨∞⟩••---

Annie Cap
United Kingdom
Author, *Beyond Goodbye: An Extraordinary True Story of a Shared Death Experience* and *It's Your Choice: Uncover Your Brilliance Using the Iceberg Process*
www.anniecap.com

In the dark days and even darker sad nights which followed the unexpected death of my mom, my life was turned upside down. After miraculously sharing in her passing, feeling her fatal symptoms as if they were my own from 5000 miles away, my senses became magnified. Unknowingly I was changed by the honor of dipping my toe into her new ethereal world, just like someone who has a near–death experience.

Seven days later, I woke up to the sensation of someone firmly touching me in the dark. I was alone in my locked bedroom (my husband was working overseas), and I was horrified by what I felt and what I expected would happen next. I was sure an intruder had en-

tered the house and was about to attack me. Afraid of whom I would
see, I forced myself to turn the bedside light on and was utterly
stunned when I saw no one in my room. I checked the door and found
it undisturbed, still securely locked from the inside. I looked in all the
corners of my room and even under the bed—there really was no one
there (at least not that I could see). I tried my best to go back to sleep,
but as soon as I closed my eyes, I started to cry as I had been doing all
week since my mom died. Suddenly I felt the heavy hand stroking me
again. Someone was definitely patting my head! After a few nights of
this shocking, invisible contact, I realized it had to be my mom trying
to comfort me from beyond the grave!

Before this, I hadn't believed in an afterlife. I hadn't believed in
heaven or hell. I thought when you died, that was it and life was
simply over. I didn't even believe in God. I had rejected God long
before when I was only eight. Sadly, as well, I didn't really believe in
angels either, although I'd always wished I was wrong about them. I
remember my mom telling me how she had seen an angel when she
was very young. She was sick in bed and very close to death when it
had appeared. The angel hovered just above her within arms' reach. It
was so comforting and beautiful that she wanted to go with it wherever it wanted to take her and was surprisingly saddened when it said,
"It's not your time," before quickly vanishing.

Although the initial upset of feeling my deceased mom touching
me soon passed and I began to find the sensation soothing, for a long
time I tried to deny it had happened.

While many people would be delighted to have their perceptions
increased and to feel their departed loved ones with them, I was
shocked and confused by my new sensitivity. Feeling my mom's spirit
touching me was in direct conflict with most of my beliefs, and what it
meant about my reality was almost too frightening to consider. So
when I began feeling someone other than my mom touching me,
this time tapping or almost punching my shoulder at night, while
repeatedly announcing, "Wake up!" I decided I had to find a way to
stop it.

Everything I read said I should be calling upon my personal guardian angel and archangels to assist me. Suddenly I sincerely hoped angels were real! I read that I needed to talk to my guardian angel

regularly, as well as those spirits who were attempting to contact me. I learned I could ask the angels (and my guardian angel specifically) for protection and that I could instruct any spirits who were "bothering me" to either go away or behave in a manner that I was comfortable with. After audibly announcing my rules of engagement (as I like to refer to them) a few times to the air, I got mad one night when the persistent prodding started up again.

I jumped out of bed as soon as I felt the first hard rap on my shoulder. This time instead of feeling afraid, I was surprised that I was actually mad. Very animated this time, rather than meekly, I paced around my house, almost strutting, shouting at my guardian angel and whatever other spirits were there listening. I told my angel that I thought he or she was slacking off and not doing a very good job of protecting me. Loudly and angrily I informed the spirits, whom I felt around me and who were poking me, that unless they approached me in a non-threatening way which I would feel at ease with, they were no longer welcome in my home and would have to leave! Oddly, I recall, for some reason I was okay with spirits being in my house, as long as they didn't frighten me.

I went back to bed feeling empowered and safe, albeit silly for walking about in my underpants yelling at my guardian angel whom I wasn't even sure existed.

Later that same night I woke to a lovely feeling as if my fingers were in a cool stream on a warm summer's day. I opened my eyes and saw a gorgeous set of oversized eyes floating above my face. There was nothing else except for the two huge greenish–blue eyes separated by the air in my room. The eyes seemed sweet and loving. They were the most beautiful eyes I have ever seen. Then one of them winked at me even without a face or a nose to hold it in place. I giggled and found I felt strangely happy, so different from how I had been feeling only an hour before.

Totally awake now, I decided I needed to go to the bathroom. I opened my bedroom door and stepped out onto our upstairs landing where I saw in front of me what I knew in my heart was an angel. It was breathtaking! Filled with sparkling light and a feeling of love, it was wiggling just in front of me. The angel appeared to be made of total energy. It was like nothing I'd ever imagined. Somehow I knew I was privileged to see it and to be in its presence.

Although it didn't have a head exactly, it had what looked like a hood of energy around the area where you might expect a head to be. The angel pulsed and moved from its core. It had what I can only describe as soft, gentle, yet vibrant, rounded wave-like lightning bolts coming out in all directions from its being. They were continually moving, being pulled into its center and at the same time being extended in another direction from some other part of its body. I couldn't recognize any pattern to the movements, but it never stopped constantly changing and vibrating in this fantastic, strangely comforting way. In and out, slowly and delicately, the angel throbbed and probed the air around me with its translucent, soft tendrils of curving light. It was big, much bigger than I and extended all the way to the ceiling and beyond the landing into the air over the balustrade. Although I could see through the angel, it was filled entirely with what looked like stars glistening in colors beyond anything I'd ever seen.

I noticed that the angel didn't move away from me, and I certainly didn't want to move away from it. Its many light extensions (which could easily have been described as feathers or wings if seen from afar) touched the air around my face and body. I felt loved and supported by this action, and my eyes stayed locked on the angel the entire time, simply mesmerized by its beauty.

After a few long minutes, it began to disappear. Slowly it started to fade into nothingness, its sparkling stars being the last to go. Still twinkling on and off, hundreds of opalescent gems hung in midair even after the angel's massive, glossy body was gone. Frozen by its continued magnificence, I witnessed the departure of the angel like the vanishing memory of a spectacular firework. I was held there in awe. Its final flecks of light lingered unnaturally as if suspended by invisible strings. Then they finally dispersed by slowly dropping to the floor or evaporating in the same place where they had shimmered so beautifully only moments before.

From that night on I began to feel more comfortable about my heightened senses, knowing this fantastic being was watching over me. Amazingly I realize I have actually seen an angel—just like my mom, which is extremely rare!

I am so grateful my guardian angel recognized the desperation in my voice when I yelled for its help that night. Then knowing I needed a miracle, it decided to pleasantly wake me, lift my attitude with its stunning eyes, and then honor and impress me when it met me on the landing where it revealed its exquisiteness, its strength, and its remarkable love for me.

An Angelic Cop

Carolyn B. Coleridge, LCSW
California
www.intuitivesoulhealing.com
carcole9@hotmail.com

My mother and I share the gift of psychic awareness. We often perceive the unseen world both individually and sometimes together. Some psychologists would call this a shared delusion. I describe it as a shared gift.

The winters in Connecticut where I grew up can be extremely brutal. Snowstorms are a common occurrence throughout the winter months. One Sunday night my mother and I were driving from our Hartford business to our family home in Fairfield County. The winter storm, which had started out small, set into a full-blown blizzard as we headed down the Merritt Parkway closer to the end of our journey. The visibility ahead on the road was so poor that my mother had to eventually pull over to the shoulder to wait until she could see to drive safely. My mother breathed a sigh of relief when she was able to negotiate over to the shoulder on the slippery road without skidding. We sat there for some time to let the storm pass and to regain some visibility on the road. Unbeknownst to me, my mother said a silent prayer and called in her guardian angel for help.

After twenty minutes or so, she was able to see better to drive home safely, but the snow had been coming down so fast though that it had entrapped us by the side of the road. We were stuck in a gully with the snow holding our tires captive. As many times as my mother tried to accelerate the car, the tires just kept spinning and spinning around. A chill of fear fell upon us inside the car because the parkway was often abandoned at that time of night. In fact we had not seen any cars on the highway for quite some time.

I began to ask my mother if we should call AAA for help when bright lights suddenly appeared behind us abruptly breaking my chain of thought. The headlights appeared out of nowhere! As we looked up, we realized it was a cop with a silent siren, but lights blinking. Within seconds the cop got out of his car and demanded strongly and sternly that my mother remove herself from the drivers' seat. The police officer then sat next to me without even saying hello. He started to move the car quickly and easily got it out of the gulley that we had spent twenty minutes stuck in.

As I stared at him, I couldn't help but notice that he sat up very straight and his skin was extremely pale. He also had no hint of facial hair and looked to me like a mannequin. There was something "unearthly and unreal" about his appearance. There also was a serene and quiet air in the car. If you have been in the presence of spirits, you know the dimensional vortex they open. This vortex brings with it a stillness and sense of peace.

As the cop got out of the car, he didn't even wait for a thank you. He just opened the door, got out, and waited for my mother to get back in. Then he commanded, "Follow me!" It appeared that he was on some kind of urgent timeline. My mother got in and was surprisingly able to easily drive back onto the parkway. The cop car left ahead of us and drove off quickly. We followed him for about fifteen seconds. He seemed to be moving so fast on a snowy, unsafe highway that it seemed unnatural. Within seconds, like a scene in a bad B movie, the dusty snow encapsulated the police car in front of us, and the car just disappeared into a snowy mist. My mother and I were silent for a while both knowing what had just occurred, but neither of us broke the silence. Then I said, "Mom," wanting to hear what my mother's thoughts were. But she interrupted me saying, "SHHH CAROLYN!" I know when these things happen words seem to ruin the moment, and my mother wanted the moment to last a little longer. It generally feels like an opening in between realms.

We drove for a while more, and then I just couldn't be quiet any longer as I blurted out, "MOM, THAT WAS AN ANGEL!" My mother with her ever-present self-assurance looked at me, responding, "Yes, when I saw the blizzard, I called in my guardian angel. I never knew he would show up as a cop!"

Pull Back a Little

Jerry E.
Michigan
danceguy2002@hotmail.com

I had just gotten into bed and rolled over to my right side. Just then my heart started beating and pumping erratically. A man suddenly appeared. He looked to be middle aged and was wearing a white shirt and tan-colored pants. This man, whom I would describe as either an angel or a spirit, suddenly slipped down in front of me. By this I mean that he was horizontal as I was. His head faced me, and his body, like mine, was facing up.

He lifted his right arm and pointed behind me with his right index finger and said, "Pull back a little." When he did this, his entire right forearm, hand, and finger enlarged considerably. I suspect this was so I would understand his meaning even if I possibly didn't hear what he said. His arm and finger made it impossible for me to miss his meaning. I definitely would have understood and moved back even if no words were spoken.

With these words, he was instantly gone, and I laid there momentarily thinking, *Why should I pull back?* For an instant I thought, *Hell, I'm not going to do it.* But then it occurred to me that I might as well pull back because it wouldn't hurt anything and so I moved back a couple of inches.

My heart instantly returned to beating and pumping normally. It was at this moment that I realized what had just happened: I had been paid a visit by a divine being. Whether he was an angel or a spirit, I am totally convinced that he saved my life, allowing me more time on this earth plane. It was not my time to go.

Thinking back, he looked like just a normal guy except for the fact that he was enclosed in a whitish haze like a fog. Even with all the whiteness around him, I could tell that his hair was also white. His face was very pale—so pale, in fact, that I couldn't tell whether he was clean shaven or had any facial hair. Having this experience was personal proof that we continue to have very active lives after we die.

A Prayer to Sai Baba of Shirdi

Vandana Ritik Mulchandani
India
www.saivandana.blogspot.com
vandana.mulchandani@gmail.com

Sai Baba of Shirdi was an Indian fakir or guru whom many regarded as a saint and still do. In fact, even though his spirit left his body in 1918, Sai Baba called himself the messenger of God and continues to have millions of followers and devotees worldwide.

To me God is One, but we call him by different names and worship him in many ways. How we worship doesn't matter, however, because the only thing that matters is that we have a single-minded belief in whomever we believe to be the symbol of God. Having said this, I have had many mystical experiences as a result of my devotion to Sai Baba whose spirit I believe is present all around me. I personally believe that he is my guardian angel or ascendant master. Whatever name is used doesn't matter. What does matter is that I see all in him and him in all.

Sai Baba said that if devotees have faith in him, he would cross even seven seas to fulfill their desires. I would like to share one such experience in which Sai Baba was there for me. Some years ago a group of us had arranged for a mass feeding of the poor, mostly beggars and lepers at Lodhi Road Saibaba Temple in New Delhi, India. Deep down inside I wanted Sai Baba himself to be part of our efforts to feed the poor.

Before we started distributing the food packets, we had gone to the temple wherein I mentally prayed to Sai Baba for his blessings during our humble effort. I was also thinking, *Sai Baba, can you come today? It would be nice. But please do not come in the form of a beggar or leper. You are the Giver to all so how can you come in this form? Even though you have taught me to see God in all and treat all equally, I will not like it if you come as a leper or a beggar. I will not be able to recognize you and could miss you.* I then left the temple and forgot about my request as I went about the day.

Later as we were distributing the packets outside, all the people were coming in a queue taking their goodies and walking away. At the end of it all, we were satisfied that we had given to all who had wanted food and still had some packets to spare.

There was no line now, but I suddenly saw a tall, thin, healthy-looking man walking towards us, dressed simply and informally in a white and yellow cotton dress. He did not seem to be in need of any free food. Still he came over to us and said he wanted to have lunch. When he saw us picking up a food packet, he refused to take it, saying, "I am not a beggar. I am a Pandit (priest). I want food to be served to me in a proper manner, otherwise I do not want it."

To satisfy this man, we offered him a proper takht (wooden bed) to sit on under a tree, and we arranged for a proper plate to serve him the food with some additional dishes of his choice. He ate comfortably and even asked for water (we had not served water with the food packets) and later asked for some dakshina (cash offering). We gave him water but were a bit reluctant to offer money since we had not offered it to others. He did not say a word in response and simply walked away. Seconds later I changed my mind and decided to give him some money. I rushed off to find him, but he was nowhere to be found. He had disappeared within seconds.

At the time I was confused by what had taken place and did not realize what had truly happened. Later that day when the food distribution was finished, I drove back to my office in somewhat of a daze when I suddenly woke up and everything became so clear. *Oh, my God,* I thought. *How ignorant and foolish of me!* I thought of my private prayer and request earlier that day. Sai Baba had come in the form of a priest as per my request. It didn't even strike me when he categorically clarified that he was not a beggar. I had said that I would not like it if he came as a beggar and he followed my wishes.

When I reached the office, I told my friend what had happened. My friend replied by telling me that when God comes to us, we lose our senses of logical thinking. If I had understood right then and there that this man was Sai Baba, things would have been much different. But perhaps things happened just as they were meant to happen. My wish to Sai Baba was fulfilled, and as a result, I received proof that the Universe answered my prayers in a way that I would understand.

Luckily for me this was not the only divine encounter I experienced. I am an early riser and love to get up at 4 a.m. since this is the time, per ancient Hindu scriptures, during which all good angels are near the earth's realm. As part of my early morning ritual, I wake up and walk over to an altar in my living room and wish, "Good Morning," to the Universe. This is an altar where I pray to God and keep pictures there of some great souls including Sai Baba, Jesus, Mary, etc.

Sometimes it is difficult to get up so early, but I always set my alarm clock on my mobile phone and force myself to get up despite how sleepy or tired I may feel. On this particular morning I had woken up just a few minutes before my 4 a.m. alarm. As I made my way over to the altar, I was distracted by some noise outside. I walked up to the front door to investigate and saw that it was just a neighbor loading luggage into his car. I then turned around wondering why I had even wasted my time and heard my cell phone beep indicating that I had a new text message. I wondered who had sent me a text message at exactly 4 a.m. The sender was unknown to me, and when I opened the message, it read, "Good Morning!"

At this moment I realized that I had forgotten to wish good morning to the angels and the Universe. This was God's way of letting me know that He was aware of my wishes. WOW! I was so excited because I knew my good intentions were being acknowledged in a powerful way.

Throughout that day I couldn't help feeling excited about what had just occurred. Later that evening I decided to call the sender of the text message. The stranger immediately apologized telling me that he had accidently pressed the wrong digit. He had intended the message, he explained, for his girlfriend.

There are no accidents. What are the odds that I would get this exact and precise two word message at the most opportune time? The message was sent at exactly 4 a.m. I have no doubt that God and his angels prompted this stranger to press the wrong button, thereby sending me this message. Thankfully I got it. Angels are all around us and make their presence known to us in one form or another. We need only believe.

The Third Man

Lance Beem
California
lancebeem@kbrfoundation.org

Several years ago I was traveling in my blue pickup truck from Salinas Valley over to the Central Valley of California. Just before I came to the beginning of the mountain pass that leads into the Central Valley, I saw suddenly without warning in a quick flash the vision of my front windshield shattering and my body going through it. I saw blood and glass everywhere as a result of this image in my mind of a horrific and deadly impact.

Stunned by what I had just seen vividly in my mind, I tried to shake it off and clear my head of that terrible feeling. I could not help but think immediately what would happen to my wife and daughter should something like this happen to me. However, almost as quickly as this vision came, my thoughts were interrupted again because within the next ten seconds, an oncoming red pickup truck suddenly veered into my lane. The truck was traveling towards me in the on-coming lane, head on, at about 60 mph with three men in the front cab. As the vehicle approached me, I could literally see the whites of their wide-open eyes. The driver and right window side passenger appeared to be of darker Hispanic complexion with black hair. The man sitting in the center between them was of a lighter complex-ion with a thin long nose, tan face, a beard, and long brown hair. He was wearing what appeared to be a white shirt. It was like a snapshot of them in front of me. I will never forget it.

At this moment I was very alert and tense because of the vision of that terrible accident I had just visualized moments earlier in my mind. As the red truck came at me head on, I knew without a moment's hesitation, as I had done this a hundred times before, to pull immediately and flawlessly hard to the right. It was just as I was supposed to do this . . . like my hands were being guided naturally. I was like someone on autopilot who knew exactly what to do to avoid the impact. My quick actions took me down a steep incline off the shoulder of the road. As I was going down, I glanced at my right side mirror and saw that the pickup truck had flipped. Apparently it had flipped more than once, catapulting the driver out into the freshly disked vegetable field.

It is rare in this expensive vegetable growing region of high farm land values that a field remains unplanted for more than a few days. If the field had been planted, the field surface would have been com-pacted and hard. That day was a lucky one for the driver as he landed on a soft bed of dirt after he had been thrown from the driver's seat.

As my truck continued going down, my body bumped all over the place until I got to flat ground. My truck stalled, and I just thought, *Wow*. Then without thinking I turned the key and started my truck up again, making my way up and across the highway. The driver in the vehicle behind me did the same. We ran out of our vehicles in an attempt to help these guys quickly. We found the one Hispanic pas-senger who was wearing a blue flannel shirt was in shock, moaning, and pinned between a metal fence post and the seat as the truck was now lying on its right side. It was truly amazing because the metal fence post had him pinned inside the vehicle without piercing him like a spear. That he was alive was all I needed to know for the moment.

I then ran out into the field to help the driver who was thrown at least fifty feet from the vehicle and was now standing up. Completely disoriented, he was moaning in pain with cuts and a dislocated shoulder. I got him to sit back down in the soft dirt and thought at that moment how lucky he had been that they had disked the field. A short time later an ambulance arrived where upon two paramedics attended to the two men. Minutes later, we began to hear moaning sounds coming from the metal barbed wire fence the red pickup truck was lying on. We searched with the highway patrolmen in the tall, dry, grassy weeds along the fence line, guided by the sound of his moans.

The officers had arrived about five minutes after the paramedics. Lying face down and not moving was what I thought now to be the third man. I did not really think much about the fact he was much more heavyset than I had seen. I just guessed then that this was the third passenger seated in the middle, as he was face down in the weeds, but of course it was not, as I would find out later.

All three men were attended to and taken to the local hospital. I gave my information as a witness to the officers and then traveled over the mountain pass back home. That night I called the hospital near the accident and was told by the nurse they were all recovering and were all doing okay. I was glad it had ended the way it did; no one was killed and in every sense in my body I was grateful as I looked at my family sitting in the living room.

To my surprise more than a year later I was asked to give a deposition about the accident in the town of Hollister. As I walked in to the attorney's office, I saw two of the men who were in the front cab (the driver and window side passenger) in the waiting room. They looked at me and nodded. After the deposition I felt as if they were the ones being sued.

As it turned out, I learned from the attorney that the red pickup truck was actually towing another vehicle with a bumper-to-bumper tow hitch. It was then I remembered that day I had seen a red sedan partially sitting in the field. It turns out, they said, that the third man had been driving this red sedan attached to the bumper tow hitch behind the red pickup truck, and it loosened, causing the truck to be thrown into my lane. They said this third man was at the wheel of the second car (the red sedan) being towed when it detached. Instead of tying the steering wheel, they had this third guy holding the wheel and sitting in the towed vehicle's driver seat, which, of course, is illegal.

At the disposition, because I was sure the third man was in the middle seat in the red truck, apparently my testimony was messing up the lawsuit. The attorney was very upset and kept getting up into my face and cursing at me saying things like, "Why do you keep saying the third man was in the pickup truck? That is not what you saw; you are mistaken (intimidating me all the way)." He said, "The third man was driving the second car; there were only two men in the truck." It was an hour-long shouting match as the lawyer told me to swear that I was telling the truth which I did without hesitation. He demanded to know what my motive was to screw up everything by telling a complete lie and by saying that there were three men in the front seat of a two-door red pickup truck. I just couldn't because I saw what I saw—three men in the front seat of the pickup truck. I suspected perhaps there was scam going on here.

I was sure of what I had seen, however, and persistently kept describing the man in the middle. The lawyer came back with, "No! No! No! That was not him!" To this I kept repeating, "Well, that's what I saw . . . a lean man with a pointed noise and tanned face in a white shirt." I had no reason whatsoever to lie and was both adamant and confident about what I had seen. Truthfully I did not know that there was another guy sitting in the towed vehicle until the deposition. I thought it was all a con. At the accident scene we had found only three men.

Afterwards as I was leaving, I came back out into the lobby and now I saw this short, heavyset Hispanic man in the waiting room with crutches and his leg in a brace. He was with his wife and the other two men were gone. At that moment I remembered him (because of his size and dark hair) lying along on the fence line. It was then that I began to doubt myself and realized that this man could not have been the one sitting in between the other two men in the front cab. It also dawned on me that I had not seen the bearded man with the white shirt at the scene of the accident.

Of course, I could not now go back in and explain this to the howling attorney. How was I going to explain that the third person I had seen was actually, well, not there. How was I going to explain that the third person that I was referring to was actually someone completely different from the man I had just seen in the waiting room? I often wonder why none of us were killed that day. I can only say that none of us were meant to leave this earth then. And, today, if you were to ask me who I think the mysterious bearded man was with the white shirt, I can positively tell you that I now know that he was not there when the officers arrived. He must have been what we hear about as a spirit guide or an angel. I also wonder remembering that moment of seeing the whites in their eyes like a snapshot . . . He looked very much like the pictures I've seen of Jesus. But who am I to say?

I Was Not Alone

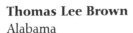

Thomas Lee Brown
Alabama

In October 1997 I was traveling home one evening from work. It was about 6:20 p.m. and it had just started raining. I had gotten to a hilltop when I noticed a vehicle traveling towards me at a high rate of speed. Still at a distance but getting ever so close, I changed lanes to avoid the car hitting me.

Imagine my surprise when the car then changed lanes and again headed straight at me. I quickly changed back to the lane I had first moved from with the other car again moving with me. I decided then that I was not going to prevent the collision so I gripped the steering wheel, hit the brakes, shut my eyes and cried out, "Dear Jesus!" . . . As the vehicle hit me head-on moving at approximately 85 mph, I felt something holding around me. It was like a great big hug. Then everything went blank and I passed out.

When I woke up, I was lying half way out of my vehicle on the other side of the highway. Someone, whom I did not know whether was male or female, was sitting with me, shielding me from the rain and assuring me that help would soon come. My motor and transmission were resting on my legs inside the car, and I could not move. I then passed out again. When I woke up, there were multiple fire fighters, medics, and police officers trying to free me from the car.

They eventually extracted me from the car and rushed me to the hospital where it was found that my hips and pelvis had been crushed and that I had a hematoma (bleeding) on the left side of my brain. The young man driving the other vehicle had died immediately, and his passenger had received injuries but lived to tell investigators that they were trying to play "Chicken" with people.[6] I later was told that my seatbelts detached with my car door when it was ripped open on impact. So no safety devices were there to hold me in. Medical personnel were surprised that I lived.

I soon recovered from many surgeries and am back 100 percent now. After my recovery, I wanted to thank the person who stayed by my side until rescue arrived but later learned that no one was there when a police officer found us. I can remember the comforting voice as if it were yesterday but cannot describe the person's look. This is when I realized that I had an angel caring for me.

---

[6]**Author's Note:** Chicken is a game in which two drivers purposefully drive towards each other. One driver must swerve or someone may die. If one driver swerves and the other does not, that driver is called a chicken and loses the game.

An Ecounter with Archangel Michael

Jose L. Adame
California
HLNHNZ@yahoo.com

One day out of the blue my wife, who was psychic, told me that she had a lump in her back. "It's a tumor," she said, "and you are going to heal me of it." To say the least I was dumbfounded by her words. At that point I had been practicing Reiki for about two years. Reiki is basically a Japanese technique where you guide life force energy to heal the body. So although I was definitely a believer in energy healing, I didn't know what to think. When my then wife said this to me, I thought, *Okay, what has she been smoking?*

But when she asked again saying, "Don't you want to help me?" I figured it couldn't hurt to try. So even though I was thinking, *Yea, right,* inside, I set up the massage table which I used for Reiki, and my wife lay down on the table. I sat by her head and began channeling Reiki. After just a few minutes, I realized that I was actually outside of my body standing by her side at the left side of the table—that is I had an outer body experience (OBE) and was actually watching myself sitting by my wife's head.

Soon I noticed that we were not alone. Standing over my wife's right shoulder was a man wearing the prettiest blue suit with a white shirt. Intuitively I sensed that he was an angel who had come to assist me. As I stared at him, I couldn't help but notice that he had the most beautiful blue eyes. The best way to describe him is to simply say that everything about him was beyond perfect.

Finally, I asked him, "What are you doing here?" He looked at me and replied, "You are going to take it out, and I will take it away." I was not surprised at all by this and simply told him that I would need a white cloth. In response he presented me with the most striking white washcloth I've ever seen. I took the cloth from him and instinctively held it up to my mouth. I then regurgitated into the cloth an egg-sized, bloody, puss-dripping tumor looking thing and wrapped it up. This all took place in the spirit plane outside of my body.

I then handed the tumor to Michael. Yes, I somehow automatically knew his name was Michael. He then disappeared, and I was left there back in my body, sitting and wondering what the heck just happened. Afterwards my wife was fine and just got up from the table. Thinking back, I remember we didn't say a word to each other about the experience. We simply went to bed that night without much dialogue at all.

For the next two days I couldn't stop thinking about what had happened. I kept thinking that I had truly lost my marbles and should really stop this Reiki stuff. But three days later, still unable to get what had happened out of my mind, I relayed the experience to my wife who just looked at me and said, "Yes, I know. I saw the same thing. The tumor is gone."

The angel who appeared to me that day was the Archangel Michael. Ever since I was young, I would have experiences in which I would see Archangel Michael out of the corner of my eye. I was confused back then and asked adults about what I was seeing. My uncle told me that it was just the devil trying to deceive me. I remember thinking, *Am I such a bad person that the devil would want to do this?*

I often wonder how different my life would have been had I accepted Archangel Michael's help much sooner, but I am truly blessed. These days I call on him for assistance, and he has worked with me on many other occasions to help and heal others. He continues to work through me and deserves all the credit.

Meeting My Master Spirit Guide

---••◁∞▷••---

Freddie Rivera
New York
http://mediumfreddierivera.wordpress.com
freddierivera718@gmail.com

I was born and raised in Manhattan, New York City and I presently live in Queens. I have always been a psychic medium, and as a child I was always terrified. I saw things and experienced a lot that I didn't understand.

This story is about me meeting my master spirit guide for the first time and the message that changed my life. I have read books by other mediums and a lot don't meet their master spirit guides, but we know they are there. We might hear their names when we ask or just see a glimpse of their presence. Master spirits have been with us since we were born as they are trying to guide us. They coordinate the other guides and bring them in to help us with relationships, careers, finance, and other things in life we need help with. I have seen and communicated with one other spirit guide called Louise. Louise helps me with my mediumship; she stands by me while I am giving a reading. In mid-February 2008 I felt weird. I sensed that there were a lot spirits around me. We mediums develop our skills in order to get better at making sense of what we are receiving. Our abilities are constantly changing, and in this case I felt as if I was opening up more. I didn't know what was coming yet, but I sure felt it. One evening my mother and I ate dinner, and after I cleaned up the kitchen, I then decided to watch television. It came time to get ready to go to bed so I brushed my teeth and washed my face. I always pray before I go to bed. I hopped in bed facing up trying to get comfortable.

About five minutes went by when I suddenly started to see faces, lots of them. It was like a slide show—some in color, black and white, or outlines of faces. I opened my eyes in amazement and confusion. I stood up on my bed wondering what was going on here. But I wasn't scared as I thought that something new was happening to me, a change. I lay back down and it began again. I just stayed there experiencing this phenomenon. I would see women, men, and children—some smiling, some serious, and some I couldn't make out. It was all so fast, and while this was happening, I didn't hear anything—no voices or anything at all. I was mesmerized, and then I slowly fell asleep.

I got up early the next morning, made a cup of coffee, sat by my computer, and lit a cigarette. (Today, I don't smoke anymore.) All day long I was in limbo with only the thought of what had happened the night before. It was time to go to bed again. I did what I normally do every night; I said my prayers and got into bed. Some time had passed when suddenly I began to see the slide show of faces again; this time I just laid there amazed at what I was seeing. I become curious, and I decided to do a test. When I opened my eyes and closed them again, it kept happening as face after face came in.

This next experience I had was truly strange. During one of my tests, I opened my eyes and caught what looked like a green fluorescent light moving about on my bed's headboard. I looked around to see if the light was coming from somewhere else; the shades were closed, and there was no way a light like that could get in. The light just moved slowly as if it had a mind of its own; it wasn't a straight light because it kept curving as if it wanted me to notice it. I didn't feel threatened or afraid at all; I felt I was being made not to feel afraid, I felt at peace, and suddenly I felt sleepy. It was like a feeling of "don't worry, it will be fine, now go to sleep" and I did. I began to feel as if there was a purpose to what was going on and I was right.

This was the night that changed my life forever. I went to bed, and again the faces came in. I was getting use to the faces, and for some reason I looked forward to it. I lay there and then turned to face my living room. I could see the living room from my bed. Suddenly I got the urge to open my eyes, and I stared directly toward the living room as I was made to do so. Suddenly I began to see a figure appear slowly; this figure was squatting down on one knee. It started to become clearer to me; I could make out the figure now; I wasn't scared. I felt at peace just as when I had seen the green hue on my bed's headboard. The figure resembled an East Indian man dressed in white; he had a small turban on his head. I kept my eyes glued to this apparition as he was transparent and not fully solid. He looked at me and smiled. I felt in my mind that he was talking to me in a telepathic way; he was conveying to me that he is my master spirit guide and that his name is Andreas.

I lay there just staring at him with a long concentrated look. I was excited, and he telepathically calmed me down. He was trying to convey something to me, and I felt as if something opened up in me. I was so calm that I turned over and fell asleep. Now when I think about this, I feel that was a bit rude of me.

When I got up in the morning, I thought about what had happened. I went to the kitchen to make myself a cup of coffee, turned on my computer to check my email, and lit a cigarette as I always did. When I turned my head towards the living room, Andreas was still there, crouching down on one knee with a smile. After a few minutes I began to feel serene, and I didn't feel that this entity was evil in anyway. Andreas told me again telepathically, as he had done the night before, that he was my master spirit guide and that I shouldn't be afraid. I then became more interested in what he had said about being my master spirit guide. He said, *I am always with you, but I am appearing to you now because you are in need, in need of knowing the truth.* I asked him, *What truth, what is it I need to know?* Andreas wouldn't answer me because I needed to find out for myself, and he didn't want to influence me.

A week went by and Andreas was still with me. He always stayed in the living room, and it was a bit unnerving to see him there all the time. I felt as if I was always being watched. We are truly never alone as I have grown to know.

I am writing an autobiography, and there is a lot more to this story. To make a long story short, my purpose here is to tell about my divine visit. Andreas was letting me know that things in my life as a medium would change, and they truly have changed. He told me that I was ready and that I will give healing to many and will bring closure to those that need it. What he said has come to pass; I have been helping those who grieve the loss of a loved one. With evidential proof I maintain that we simply don't die. I had never used my gifts in a professional manner before, but after Andreas's visit, I now do. I always asked God why I was here and what was my purpose. Andreas answered that for me. Andreas doesn't show himself to me anymore, but I know that he is there always.

The Angel Paintings

Russ Stiver
North Carolina
chasingshadows10@yahoo.com

My mother was very spiritual and believed in reading Tarot cards; she even experimented with different herbs for medicinal and health purposes. So each year she loved to attend a popular psychic fair held in the town of Warren, Ohio.

When I was about thirteen years old, my mother took a good friend of hers and me to this fair. The place was filled with various psychics vying for attention and vendors selling their mystical wares. One vendor really intrigued us, and we stopped to have a closer look. We found a table set up with a bunch of different angel paintings ranging anywhere from small (3x5) to large (20x24) prints. For some reason, I was interested and asked the vendor to tell us about them.

The paintings, we were told, were by a famous artist named Andy Lakey. Ironically he had had no formal training and had never wanted

147

to be an artist. In fact, he sold cars for a living and used his money to buy drugs. On December 31, 1986, he overdosed while at a New Year's Eve party and nearly lost his life. Knowing that he was in trouble, he prayed to God to spare his life. In return he promised to do something to help others.

Lakey had a near–death experience which led to him being visited by seven angels. After he recovered, he completely stopped taking drugs and began painting the angels whom he claimed had visited him that night. He vowed he would paint 2,000 angel portraits and has since kept that promise.

Going back to the fair, I listened intently as the vendor told us about this man whom I had never heard of at the time. The paintings, we were told, were said to give off angelic energy to anyone who touched them. Honestly, as young as I was, I thought this sounded a bit crazy. I mean a painting that gives off angel energy? That sounded like a stretch to me.

My mother and her friend picked up a portrait but said they didn't feel anything. I then followed by picking up another painting but didn't feel any sort of energy either. Truthfully, I can't say I expected to feel anything.

But about twenty minutes after leaving this booth, my hands began to hurt me. I didn't know what was going on and complained to my mother who came over to take a look. She was shocked to find that my hands had become severely swollen. I could barely make a fist, let alone bend them.

Naturally my mother was very upset, and we went back to the booth selling Lakey's angel paintings. My mother demanded to know what was on the paintings that could have done this to my hands. In response, she was told that I had probably absorbed all the energy from one of the paintings. She was not satisfied with that answer and was understandably very irate and angry.

I was taken to the hospital and a bunch of allergy tests were done on me, but nothing came back positive. The doctors had no idea what had caused me to have this kind of a reaction. To this day we still don't know what happened to me that day at the fair. While I'm not sure if I did absorb some kind of angel energy from one of Andy Lakey's paintings, I do know that it had never happened before and hasn't happened since.

So while I definitely can't prove what exactly happened that day, I do have to admit that the experience was quite a coincidence. I have heard that the angels are always around us. Perhaps they were just trying to get my attention that day. If so, it worked!

An Angel on Route 13

Barbara Wiley
Pennsylvania

I remember that night as if it were yesterday. It was a warm June evening, and I was on my way to school as I was taking night courses and working towards an associate's degree. As I headed down Route 13 towards Bristol, Pennsylvania, my tire suddenly blew out and I found myself struggling to maintain control of my car.

After I finally and successfully maneuvered it to the side of the road, I got out of the car and opened the trunk to grab my tools and the spare tire. I realized that I unfortunately didn't have a jack. A nice couple stopped to help, but they didn't have one either and soon departed, leaving me alone, angry, and almost in tears.

Out of nowhere, a man appeared behind me telling me that he had seen my tire blow out and wanted to know if I was alright. After I told him that I was indeed okay, he told me that he had a jack (he was holding one in his hand) and was going to help me put on the spare.

Thinking back, I wonder how this man just happened to have a jack in his hand. How did he know I needed one?

After he put the tire on my car, he informed me that I needed air in my spare and should get to the nearest station. I thanked him, got in my car, and drove away not seeing this kind man get into any vehicle or even seeing where he went. It was as though he just disappeared.

I drove to the nearest service station and proceeded to add air to my tire. When I turned around, there he was again as though he appeared out of thin air. I was flabbergasted as he told me he just wanted to make sure once again that I was alright. I, once more, got in my car and did not see this man get into any vehicle. In fact, there were no other cars around. How he could have gotten from the other side of the highway (where my tire blew) to this gas station in such a short span of time was logically impossible.

There were no other cars around when he had helped me with my spare. There is also a concrete median dividing the highway that goes on for miles with no intersections. How did he get from point A to point B so quickly?

All of these things didn't hit me until the next day when I realized that this man had to be an angel. I am convinced that angels do sometimes come to help those in need. I remember that even the air seemed to change when this man showed up. The noise of the traffic around us diminished, and it was almost as if time stood still.

Truthfully, I did not realize that I was standing before an angel that night until later when I reflected on the whole experience. But I like to think that this is the way it was meant to be.

My Final Goodbye

---··◁∞▷··---

Celeste
Maine

Three years ago as my father lay dying after a six-month battle with pancreatic cancer, my family gathered together at his bedside. We had all traveled from our hometown of Maine to the beautiful Gulf Coast where my parents had been spending their winters for the last twenty years. They were due to return home earlier in the month, but my father was just too sick to travel so my family and I made our way to him.

They owned a condo on a beautiful white sand beach, and they both so enjoyed spending part of their retirement there. My father once told me that he saw the face of God on that very beach. So I have no doubt that his choice would have definitely been to leave this world in that exact spot.

Days passed as my father continued to worsen, and finally the day came when I had to return to Maine. At this point, my father was in a

153

semicoma, and the pain of knowing that I had to leave him was ago-
nizing. Nonetheless, I had no choice. I had to say my final goodbye.
On this day I was giving my father his daily bed bath with my
mother and sister. We were trying to turn him over to wash and pow-
der his back, but we were having difficulty moving him. In tears and
frustrated, I quickly glanced up at the bedroom doorway and saw
whom I believed to be my brother-in-law passing by. I called out to
him to please lend us a hand.

At the time I didn't think about the fact that the person I had just
seen in the doorway was dressed all in white. My brother-in-law was
the only other person in the condo with us that day. He had been
sleeping in a spare bedroom, and I was confused as to why he didn't
answer my cry for help and come into my father's bedroom. I wondered why he had just quietly and smoothly walked past the doorway
without even saying a word or looking in. Another thing that struck
me as odd at the time was the fact that the only thing in the direction
where my brother-in-law was headed was the sliding glass doors
which led to a patio leading to the beach.

After we finished with my father, I went to gather my things to get
ready to leave for the airport. At this point my sister Michele told me
that her husband had not gotten out of bed yet that morning and was
still asleep. I was baffled. Who then was that tall person dressed all in
white who had slowly glided passed my father's door?

I was forced to temporarily put it out of my mind because I was
devastated by having to say what I knew would be my last goodbye to
my father. It was by far the hardest thing that I have ever had to do.

Later as I sat on that plane flying back home to Maine, I realized
that this was an angel. I knew that Jesus had sent an angel to carry my
father to heaven. Looking back I'm not exactly sure why I was allowed
to see this angel on that day. Perhaps it was out of compassion for me
or maybe it was to let me know that my father would be okay.

What I knew at that moment and what I know now, however, is
that my dad was with God. I will never doubt the kindness and power
of Jesus and his angels. My father took his last breath the next day, but
he was not alone.

God Works in
Mysterious Ways

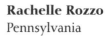

Rachelle Rozzo
Pennsylvania

I needed to make a quick stop at my doctor's office to pick up a physical paper that my daughter needed for school. A friend of mine had been having some personal problems, and I asked her to take a ride with me just to get her out of the house for a while. On our way to the doctor's office, we were in a deep discussion about God and how he gives us signs all the time that he's with us.

When we arrived, I pulled into the parking lot and drove to the spot where I normally park. I shut off the car and was about to open my door when my car drifted forward and over a rounded curb and into the yard. The curb is there to stop this from happening, yet my car decided to roll about six inches and over a curb while it was in park. I thought this was odd but considered that maybe I had just driven up too far. I picked up the papers I needed and came back out to get my car off the curb.

My car sits very low to the ground so when it went over, the bottom of my car got stuck on the curb. There was no backing it out without some sort of help. My friend tried pushing it, but she is very tiny and doesn't have much strength. I decided to get the jack out of my trunk in the hopes that I could jack the car up and possibly drive it out. At this point I didn't care about the jack getting ruined.

As I was pulling it from my trunk, my finger got pinched in the jack and chopped off a pea-sized portion of the tip of my finger. I got a bandage from the doctor's office and went back out to work on the car. The jack didn't help one bit, and my friend didn't have the strength to even budge the car although she was trying very hard.

Suddenly, a car pulled into the lot from the same direction we came. The driver stopped his car next to us, and in an unfamiliar accent said, "NO! NO! NO! Stop! I'll help you." So we stopped what we were doing and watched as he got out of his car. The man looked to be in his 70s. He was very tall with piercing blue eyes and gray hair. He spoke sternly, but softly telling my friend to stand next to him and push.

He kept telling her, "Push! Push!" But it was clear that my friend just couldn't do it. Then amazingly he lifted my car up and pushed it backwards as though it were made of light weight plastic. I remember standing there thinking, *This man has super human strength, especially for his age.* I got out of my car, saying thank you. I then told him that I loved him and gave him a hug. In response, he just patted me softly on the back with open hands as though it made him uncomfortable and then walked over to his car, got in, and left the same way he came.

My friend and I just stood there in silence for a moment looking at each other completely confused. Why did this man go back the same way he came from without even going into the doctor's office? You can't see the parking lot unless you're almost past the entrance so he couldn't have seen us before he pulled in. Why, then, was he there if he didn't have to go into the doctor's office?

We got back into the car and kept thinking about how he could have known that we needed help. Where did he come from? We were both thinking the same thing—he was an angel. I told my friend it was meant for her and she agreed. I told her that he was there to tell her that she needed to push to get her life in order. He was there to give her the faith she so desperately needed. For weeks afterwards my friend couldn't get this man out of her head and strongly believes he was only there to restore her faith.

God works in mysterious ways. This day he sent an angel to show my friend that she needs to fight to get her life in order and possibly to slow us down so we could avoid a tragic accident. It also amazed me how quickly my finger healed. It was completely healed within four days to the point where you would have never known I had even injured it. I could literally watch it healing. Again, God certainly does work in mysterious ways.

Your Grandpa Is Going to Be Fine

Anonymous
California

My grandfather was a wonderful man whom my family and I loved very much. When he was diagnosed with colon cancer, it was tough on all of us and we wanted to be there for him. It was difficult at times, however, because he lived in Oregon—ten hours away from my home in California. When he was nearing the end of his time here on earth, my mom and her sister drove up to be with him.

Even though I wasn't there in person, I was there in spirit as he was in my thoughts and in my heart. My grandmother had asked me and the rest of the family to pray for him and we did. I prayed on my knees and was in tears as I asked God to help and protect my grandfather. I asked, for example, that he guide him to the Other Side. I even asked the help of my angels and spirit guides ending with the saying "God's will be done." My grandfather passed a few days later.

I don't remember if my divine encounter occurred on that same night or if it was the day after my grandfather had crossed over, but I had a vivid dream in which an angel visited me in my sleep. I was taken to a place. I couldn't see who this person was guiding me on this journey, but I could feel a presence on my right side. We ended up in a beautiful, glowing white place. As I write this now, my nose is tickling like crazy. I know this is a sign that angels or spirit guides are here with me now. This place was so incredibly real and in many ways incomparable or indescribable. As we got closer and closer to this place, I noticed that there was a man kneeling and waiting for me. I can still see him in such detail. He was glorious and shone with this magnificent white light. It was almost as if he was reflecting the sun in the same way the moon does.

This man had blond hair and appeared to be of average height. He had no facial hair and was the age of a young man in his prime. The white robe he wore glowed with brilliant white light just as he did. As I stood there before him, I felt as if I knew him and I did. As I stood about five feet away from him, I sensed that he was confident, loving, and full of God's glory.

Deciding at that point to speak, I asked him if his name was Jason. I regret that I said this now, but for some reason I felt that this was one of my guardian angels named Jason. As soon as he spoke, I knew that his name was not Jason, but it didn't seem to bother him. He only laughed and chuckled with a smile and said, "Yeah."

He then spoke to me with a comforting and reassuring voice, saying, "Your grandpa is going to be fine." I smiled, lowering my head in grief, and said, "I know." Then I was suddenly awake back in my bedroom. It was as if I hadn't been sleeping at all but just daydreaming the entire thing. I instantly knew that I had been given a gift and for that I am thankful. I told my family about the dream, and it brought us all a lot of comfort in our sorrow.

About two weeks later, I found myself meeting this same angel again in my dreams. This time he had a message from my grandfather, and this time we were talking face to face as if we were old friends. If I had to describe this place the second time, I can only say that it was like being in a cloud that emanated white light. There were no walls, doors, or anything material.

Strangely, everything about it was very comfortable and familiar to me. It was as if I knew exactly where I was and had been there before. Although I felt as if I was there talking to this entity for a long time, I can recall only a brief part of our conversation. At some point he told me that my grandfather said that I was very interesting to watch. This made me both laugh and smile because it definitely sounded like something my grandfather would say. Right after I heard these words, I was immediately awake.

Thinking of this light being now reminds me of how normal he seemed and how comprehensible his voice was. He was so easy to understand and spoke with no accent just as plainly as anyone else on this earth would. Yet despite the feeling of commonality, his character was unforgettable. He spoke with the strength or knowing of an army general.

Having had these two experiences, I have no doubt that my grandfather is happy and doing well on the Other Side. And I know we will someday meet again. In the meantime, I do my best to live my life both aware and connected to the light. I am so blessed to have witnessed it.

The Voice behind Me

DeWitt
Michigan

My father had become friends with a man he worked with, and his family would often come over to our house for a visit. One day this man came over after work. He and my father talked for a while until my brother called and said he needed a ride home. My father then left to go pick him up, and his friend left with him, both driving off in separate cars.

At this time I was home alone and certainly didn't expect my father's so-called friend to return, but he did, entering through the back and cornering me in the living room. I was both surprised and shocked as he made his horrible intentions very clear. In fact, he took great pleasure in taunting me and letting me know that even if I could make it to the phone, no one, not even my boyfriend, could help me in time. I was totally terrified.

Something inside me told me to call out to God, specifically his

163

angels, for help. I was brought up believing in guardian angels and had never needed their help more than that moment. So my heart called out for assistance, and I suddenly heard a voice clearly coming from behind me. It was a man's voice; he told me to slowly walk over and pick up my father's belt which he had removed and left behind before leaving to pick up my brother.

The voice continued telling me to wrap the belt slowly around my wrist, keeping an eye on the attacker and making sure that the buckle was on the top and visible. I've often wondered why I was asked to do this. Maybe the angel knew that doing this would distract the man. At that point in my life, the belt was a symbol of discipline and my own father's authority. So perhaps it was to instill courage in me. Although I will never know for sure, these are two possibilities that come to mind.

Then the voice told me, when the right time came, I was to run for the front door and not to look back. Suddenly the attacker's eyes enlarged as though something alarmed him. His head was now angled up as though he was staring at something gigantic and very big behind me. I then realized that this was the opportune time to run and made a dash for the door.

As I ran passed him, he stood there as though he was frozen in place and couldn't move. I almost looked back but remembered the warning by the male voice not to look back and didn't. I ran to my neighbor's house as fast as I could and remained there until it was time for my little sister to arrive home by the school bus. My neighbor asked what was wrong, knowing something must have happened, but I didn't say a word. I was so afraid to tell her. The whole thing just sounded too bizarre, and I feared she wouldn't believe me.

When I finally returned to the house, no one was there. In fact, not only was it empty, but it was also very peaceful. When I later told my mother what had happened, she understandable totally freaked out. This took place in the 1960s, and back then rape was believed to be sexual and this was a taboo subject that people didn't speak of in public. So, naturally, what happened to me was denied and pushed under the rug.

Over the years I have shared my experience with very few but more recently have felt the need to share my experience. As you can imagine, it completely changed me, and I want others to be inspired and encouraged by it. I want millions to hear it and know that God and his angels are watching. I honestly don't know why my life was spared that day. I don't know why some are spared while others are not. What I do know is that this story is true.

God sent his angels to defend me when I was left totally unable to defend myself. My angel was no golden-haired damsel with flowing white wings. He was instead the height of the ceiling in our home and an adversary to be feared. He struck sheer terror into the heart of my attacker.

After my encounter, I prayed for his daughters. I knew they must have also been suffering. A few weeks after the incident, my attacker was arrested and put in jail for being the father of his daughter's baby. His daughter had become pregnant for the second time, having had a secretive abortion the first time to cover up for her father's horrendous deeds. This time around, however, the poor girl ran away, and the child was born. DNA tests proved what this man had done, and the truth was finally out, setting all his daughters free.

I truly hope that my sharing this story will bring peace and light into the lives of those who read it. People need to know that God's angels are real.

Yet Again, I Survived

Anna
South Carolina

I should have been killed a few times, but time and time again my life was spared. In fact, I was born with a very serious block of the small intestine and should have died at birth. My family had a total of eight doctors working on my case. Seven of them told my parents to make funeral arrangements because there was no hope for me. One doctor agreed to operate on me at just seven days old and miraculously I survived.

There is no doubt in my mind that I was allowed to live for a reason. In fact, I believe angels and spirit guides have been working to make sure that this purpose is fulfilled. For example, I was once in a serious car accident while driving east on Route 78 in New Jersey during the evening in the midst of traffic. Route 78 is one of the Garden State's busiest roadways. The truck I was driving rolled over three times, yet I never came out of my seat . . . even though I was not wearing a seatbelt.

Truthfully, I should have been seriously injured, if not killed, yet I was not even hurt. At the moment of impact I felt and saw what looked like a huge golden bubble wrap itself around and protect me. How is it possible to roll three times and not be ejected from your seat without a seatbelt? All I can say is anything is possible with the guidance of an angel.

On yet another occasion, I was driving on Route 287, also in New Jersey, with my then five-year-old son. Heavy snow had just started to fall, forming a slippery mess. As I neared an overpass, a car lost control ahead and other vehicles began to slam into each other. All of a sudden I felt something literally come straight through my body and grip the steering wheel. As crazy as this might sound, I was not driving! Something took control of that steering wheel helping me to avoid an eight-car pileup and escape injury. Yet again, I survived.

Over the years, I have had many spiritual and psychic experiences. I have even recalled past-life memories. When I was younger, my grandmother told me that her mother and my grandfather had the gift of sight. This is also known as the gift of second sight or being able to see with your mind's eye. Many people who have this gift can see into the future or even the past and make contact with spirits or angels.

This gift runs in my family as I also have the ability to see, hear, and feel through the veil. Truthfully we all have the ability to connect with spirit or the divine. We need only to be open to receiving and recognizing this fact. We are all spiritual beings having a human experience.

The $20 Tip

Mark Keillor
Ohio

A music lover, I've played the piano for most of my life. I would often perform in different venues in the area for extra money. On one very cold and snowy January night, I was playing at the Smith's Row Restaurant in Columbus, Indiana, for tips only. Due to the bad weather, business was really slow, and my tip jar was empty . . . except for the seed money I had put in there from my own pocket.

As the four-hour engagement went on and my back began to ache from sitting on the piano stool for so long, I began to say a short prayer. . . *It would be nice to make about twenty dollars to pay, at least, for my trip downtown.* The dining room had been almost empty all night so I was aware of every face at every table. Quitting time finally came, and I began to gather my music equipment and still no tips. As I focused on the task of gathering up music notes and equipment, I heard a voice behind me say, "I enjoyed your music." I then turned to find a sharply dressed man wearing a green pullover sweater who promptly handed me a $20 bill.

A bit taken back, I replied, "Thank you very much. I'm glad you enjoyed it." But the whole time I was looking at him and wondering where he had come from. He had not been in the dining room all evening. Of this I was certain. The man then walked out the front door about fifteen feet from where we were standing and didn't even put on a coat.

The dining room had about eighteen tables in it so I could clearly see every person at each and every table. No more than two people were seated at a table, and only about four tables were used all evening. So, again, I know this man had not been there. I also know that this man had come in answer to my prayer.

Luckily for me, this was not the only time my prayers have been answered. One summer my sister and her son Justin came to visit from Oregon. My nephew was in his mid-twenties at the time, and we asked him if there was something special he would like to do while he was with us in Southern Indiana. His reply was that he would like to attend a Chicago Cubs baseball game. Chicago is a four-hour drive from where we lived, but I also had a brother in Chicago who was able to get tickets.

At this time my son Stephen had been driving for about a year, and he quickly latched on to the idea that he could drive himself and his cousin to Chicago, meet up with his other cousin, and the three of them could have a blast at the ball game. I reluctantly agreed because it seemed like the right thing to do.

The morning of their departure, we had been hit by a mid-summer cold wave, and the rain was intense. The boys left around 7:00 a.m. in my son's Chevy S-10. I headed to a business meeting in Indianapolis that started at 9:00 a.m. About half an hour into my meeting, my cell phone rang and from the other end I heard, "Dad, the truck's not running right." The automatic transmission was not shifting into high gear, and they were racing the engine along in second gear all the way to Lafayette, Indiana, about a hundred miles away.

I was deeply involved in my meeting and not in a position to give Stephen's situation due attention, so I told him I would give it some thought and call him back. I actually didn't know what kind of thought to give it, but I knew that a prayer would be a good idea. It went like this, *Please, God, give me an idea for something to tell Stephen that will fix the truck problem so all the boys can have their fun at the ball game . . . and please don't let it look too miraculous because I don't want them to get spooked.*

The minutes seemed like hours, and then a thought came to me—electricity and water. Automatic transmissions work from electrical signals, and they were driving through a hard rain. I had to formulate a plan and come up with some words. I took a break from the meeting and called Stephen. "Have you stopped for gas yet?" I asked. "No," he said. "But we're going to have to pretty soon." "Okay," I replied. "Stop for gas and open the hood on the truck. You might have water in an electrical connection, and maybe it will evaporate out if given a chance. Call me when you are back on the road."

I went back to praying and then went back to the meeting. Luckily my part of the meeting had been completed. I looked at my watch about every thirty seconds, and about 120 glances later, my phone finally rang. "It's running fine, Dad," was music to my ears from the phone. The rest of the trip was flawless and remains one of their best memories. It remains one of my best memories as well and an event for which I still say a prayer of gratitude once in a while. Stephen is an electrician and could probably solve that problem now on his own.

.

My Present from God

---·◆◇◆·---

Lori
New York

On January 23, 1945, the state of Pennsylvania was in the midst of a severe snowstorm. And it's also the day that I decided to enter this world. At 3:33 a.m. I was born in a Catholic hospital by three nuns. My mother was alone because the doctor as well as my father could not make it up the mountain during the storm.

My mother's water never broke, and I was born in the caul (a portion of the amniotic sac which attaches to the baby as it is being delivered.) Typically a covering resembling a veil forms over the infant's face. Cauls have been the subject of many superstitions and beliefs. In biblical times if a child was born with the veil over their face or forehead, he was said to have a gift from God. After the delivery the nuns actually asked my mother if she wanted to keep the caul which can be preserved by allowing it to dry out completely. My mother opted not to keep it but always regretted this decision years later.

173

It wasn't until I grew older and started speaking that it became obvious that I was different. For example, I knew things that I shouldn't have known. The problem, however, was that I didn't realize that I was different until much later in life. I thought everyone could see what I saw. I would stand next to someone, and pictures would automatically flash before my eyes, giving me information about this person or messages from those on the Other Side. It didn't frighten me because even then I had no doubt that this was a gift from God and in fact, called it my present.

I went through my life, trying my best to fit in, but at times it wasn't easy. No one was even talking about the gift of mediumship in the 40s, 50s, and 60s. So I kept quiet about my ability and told no one.

Then when I was sixteen, I had to have my first of fifteen major surgeries because I had tumors on both sides of my lumbar spine. I asked Dr. Greco what was going to happen to me before and after the surgery. He simply explained that I was going to be given a shot of something to relax me, lifted onto a gurney, taken down to the operating room, and that I would later wake up in the recovery room. This all sounded good to me because pain and I were now very good friends. I was used to it.

Everything went as the doctor had described it except for one thing: I was above my body looking down at the scene below. I was wearing greens and hooked up to all kinds of tubes with doctors and nurses surrounding me. I could clearly hear them speaking and also heard a radio playing a Johnny Mathis song in the background. They were all frantically trying to bring me back to life as I was clinically dead. But I wasn't really dead because as I said, I was above observing the whole thing.

Thinking back, I really don't know how long this went on as there was no concept of time. Suddenly, I became aware of another reality and got to observe where I now was. The colors of the spectrum were bouncing all around my energy. There also seemed to be this gentle breeze surrounding me, both cool and warm all at the same time. Everything appeared to be soft, like rose petals. And the sound that I now heard wasn't music but a steady humming sound. (Years later I learned that this was actually the sound that the Universe makes—the ohm sound).

There were many energy beings (deceased relatives and friends) surrounding me from this lifetime and from past lives. They all seemed to know me and my energy. It was all so comforting! I have no idea how much time went by. The doctors and nurses were still working on my body below. The next thing I knew energies appeared on both my left and right side. They let me know who they were. On the left were my mother's parents and on the right my dad's. What was amazing about this is the fact that I knew them. Two had passed away before I was born, and two, I was too young to have known. But here they were. They had come to help me make the transition from my physical body to this other place.

I thought then if I could be here with all my loved ones from this lifetime and past lives, then that must mean that eventually I would also be with my parents, sister, and other relatives. We would all be together again at some point in time. Once I realized this, I didn't want to leave and telepathically communicated this by asking, *Could I please stay here with you?* An answer came back to my being, *You must go back in your body called Lori for there is something you must do. You will be back to this holding area, but you are not finished.*

Anyone who knows me will tell you that I always was a very persistent person. I don't take "no" for an answer, so I again asked: *Are you sure I can't stay in this holding area with you?* To this I again heard: *You will be back, but this wasn't supposed to happen. Go back into your body called Lori.*

Well, quite honestly, I did not know how to stay and I didn't know how to go so I just waited. They were still working on me. I don't know if three seconds, three minutes, or three hours had gone by. I don't know because everything stayed the same . . . the colors, the breeze, the sound, the softness, my loved ones, etc. But now something different was happening. My loved ones started to move over to the left or to the right; they were making a center.

I, then, remember this incredibly gigantic energy appearing before me. It was so great that it is completely indescribable. There was no question; I knew it was God. I was in the presence of God. He explained to me why I had my present. I am no better than anyone else. I have it now because I have had it before in previous lives. I wanted to learn what to do with this gift since I knew it came from God. I,

then, became a computer of information. I use this word now because
we all know what one is and can relate. But, of course, personal com-
puters didn't exist in 1961. Information was being fed into my energy.
I describe this as learning secrets. So many amazing answers were
given to me to the most complex questions I ever asked or would ever
need to ask.

When all this information stopped, I asked God a question: *What do
I do if someone asks me a question that I don't know how to answer?* God explained that all I had to do was go to my center and that the answer
would come. God also explained that we are here to learn, grow, and
teach. That everything happens for a reason, and it was all planned
out since our souls were first created.

We are all on an amazing journey. Once all of our lessons are
learned, we will be in heaven with our Creator. We begin as brand
new souls, go through many lifetimes, and end as old souls. We all
have three angels assigned to us who can take human form to keep us
on course. Free will is not what we think it is. We have a choice of one
thing and only one—the kind of person we choose to be. There is no
such thing as coincidence. We have to listen to our center and follow
the plan.

The next thing I remember about my near-death experience (NDE)
is someone calling my name, "Lori! Lori! Are you okay?" I opened my
eyes and realized that I was in recovery and that my parents were
there. I assured my parents that I was okay, but why were they asking
me this? In response, at the exact same time, they both replied, "Because you look different." I quickly replied, "OH MY GOD! I am different. I learned the secrets." They were both confused and asked me to
explain what I was talking about. I told them exactly what had happened, and they both cried. Dr. Greco did not tell them that I had died
during surgery and was brought back. No one was talking about NDE's
back then. There wasn't even a term for this type of an experience.

A short time later Dr. Greco came into the recovery room, still wearing his greens and asked how his little patient was doing. He was not
prepared for what came next. I told the doctor that I was fine but
needed to tell him something. Dr. Greco smacked his hands together
and said, "Shoot," encouraging me to continue. I went on to tell him
every last detail of what had happened right down to the Johnny

Mathis song playing on the radio. Knees buckling, Dr. Greco fell into my gurney turning as green as the greens he was wearing. My father held onto him as my mother grabbed the IV bottles; they were glass back then. Dr. Greco then told me, whispering, that he had heard two other doctors talk about such experiences over the years involving patients but that I had been his first.

Ever since my experience, I have been using my "present" to help others. I am a medium and have been channeling to bring closure to the bereaved ever since. I never charge a penny for my services because it isn't about the money and never will be. We all have a soul purpose, and this is mine.

Sidebar

Lori noted that during her near-death experience, she was given
information about things she never knew before. She was told
that she would be able to answer any question posed to her
simply by going to her center. I therefore took the opportunity
to ask Lori some pressing questions of my own. What follows
are my questions with her responses:

1. What is the purpose of life? Why are we here?

We are here to do three things: learn, grow from what we learn,
and then teach. God calls these "the lessons." Everything we do
is about some lesson that needs to be learned on this journey. (I
call it "getting the kinks out.") We have a goal, and it is called
heaven. Heaven simply means that we never have to do this
again. Our soul is now back with its Creator. God planned it this
way the second our soul was created.

2. What is the meaning of suffering?

Suffering allows us to walk in many shoes. How can one learn
true compassion if we don't feel what others feel? Those who
are uncomfortable with someone's disability or handicap
haven't experienced it. Compassionate people feel, inside their
being, what another is going through. Inside "the body" is the
soul, the essence of who we are—our center. Someone who has
gone through many lifetimes and many challenges handles adversity on a different level than one who has not had many
mountains to climb. Therefore, it is important not to meet people
from their outside. Meet their soul, and you will know the journeys that have taken place.

3. What happens when we die?

When we die, it takes one to three days for the soul to "realize"
that it is no longer in its physical body. This takes place after the
funeral or memorial service. It is somewhat earthbound because
the loved ones are around, and it has connected with familiar
energies. Once this is over, the soul goes to "the holding area."
This is where all souls dwell while waiting for loved ones who
will eventually pass over too. When we die and we go to the
holding area, we are met by these loved ones who help us make
the transition from the physical body.

4. Is there reincarnation?

There is no concept of time as we know it. Once every soul that we are waiting for passes over to the holding area, we get to move on. The soul chooses a new mother, thereby choosing a new father. They are chosen for the lessons that need to be learned by their child. Siblings choose the same parents. They are souls that were either so connected in a past life that they want to do this together again, or souls who need to work through something left undone from a past life.

5. Why does God create? Is it because he wants to or is it a necessity?

God creates for both reasons: wants to and needs to. It is almost like an experiment. Why does it take so long for some souls to "get it," and others, less time? With each lifetime that God has planned for us, we are being observed. When we die and meet with God, God's main question is: "What have you done for me?" (Meaning what have you given back or for what you have been given?) The saying goes: Every day is a gift from God. What you do with it is your gift back. That's all God is asking so that his children can learn all lessons on the journey. We begin as new souls, who know nothing, and end having learned all lessons, the main being that it is not about us—thus, old souls.

6. Is there some yet to be discovered link connecting the physical and metaphysical, such as string theory, dark matter, and energy, which science is struggling with because it doesn't conform to its expected behavior of the universe?

None of this conforms to science because it is over analyzed, over thought, no formula. Science can't say "whatever!" We humans are made up of matter, and matter is energy. Energy can neither be created nor can it be destroyed. When we die, the energy is still here, and it takes a new form. If you were to see it, you'd see hazy smoke or orbs of light (which show up in photographs!). It does things to get our attention . . . energy-related things—lights flickering, phone calls at 3 a.m. and no one there (they don't know the time!). They are just attempting to get our attention. Science doesn't know how to explain this with a formula.

7. *What is the purpose of lower life forms?*

Every life form has a purpose. So many discoveries have been made based on lower forms of life than man. God put everything on the earth that we need to sustain life. The food chain exists for a reason. Eating is survival. When a soul is going through the active process of dying, it stops eating. That's when loved ones panic because they know the end is near. So they try to make the person keep eating. But the soul is saying: I am done in this body, and it time to move on. Once we are done, that is it; this part of the journey is complete.

The Angels Are Singing to You

Vicki Lemler
Indiana
jaclem@mchsi.com

Seconds turned into minutes; minutes turned into hours. When was I ever going to get to sleep? 2:12 . . . 2:13 . . . 2:14. . .every minute for the last three hours I had seen the clock turn. I was extremely frustrated because my husband Jack (a tour bus driver) and I (a tour guide) would be getting up in just a few short hours to go on a multiday bus tour trip. I needed my sleep. And 2:15 . . . 2:16 . . . Oh, brother!

My sleepless night was like many other nights. I was very worried about my mother and couldn't sleep. She was living in a cute little two-bedroom house in Columbia City, Indiana all alone. My father had passed in 1969. She had lived there for the past seventeen years, but now it was time to find her a safer place to live. My mother was in her 80s and needed to be in a more appropriate living place.

There were just too many close calls. One day, for example, she called to tell me how she had been using her new lawn mower. She said there was a bar you needed to hold down as you held the handle. Holding the bar down caused the mower to propel itself. She was mowing her front yard, and the mower got away from her. She followed it down the sidewalk and into the street. She had forgotten to release the bar. Had she done so, the mower would have stopped.

During another incident I had received a phone call from the Columbia City Fire Department, informing me that my mother called them because her carbon monoxide alarm had gone off. They told me she did the right thing by calling them, but then she just sat down in her living room to wait for them. Obviously she should have gone outside. The firemen waited there with my mother until I arrived and then suggested that I take her to the hospital. I did and she was given oxygen.

Each day was turning into a cross-your-fingers-and-pray sort of day. I also worried because her washer and dryer were in the basement. Those steps were more than she could handle. I always worried about the possibility of her falling and then finding her at the bottom of the steps. And so the clock continued 3:15 . . . 3:16. . . 3:17 . . . I would never forget this night; it was June 25, 2004. It was now nearly 3:30 in the morning, and I was utterly exhausted. Without realizing it I had almost fallen into a comfortable and much-needed sleep. I had just reached those few seconds just as your eyes close and your body relaxes. And then it happened. I heard the most beautiful music I have ever heard in my life.

There were no words or instruments, just the most astounding, unbelievable melody of voices. It sounded like hundreds of beautiful voices singing "ah." I opened my eyes then totally awake. I looked around the room and then at my husband before staring out the window at the many breathtaking stars in the sky. All the while the incredible music continued and was coming from outside my mind. I could literally hear the music along with the cars going by and everything else that was happening at the moment. My whole being filled with such awe that I felt humbled and privileged. My eyes swelled with tears.

When I was in high school, we would sing the "Hallelujah Chorus" by Handel. Doing so would always put a lump in my throat and tears

in my eyes. I was so incredibly moved by both the music and the
words. But there was absolutely no comparison to what I was listening
to on this night. Whatever it was far exceeded the Handel feeling a
hundred times over. I truly felt I was experiencing the most wonderful
gift. In my mind and not through spoken words, I asked myself: *What
is this?* A very low, deep, male voice spoke with such kindness and love
immediately responded, "The angels in heaven are singing to you." It
was as though he was sitting right there next to me talking. I did not
disbelieve. Only angels could produce something so perfect and so
full of love.

And this is exactly what I was feeling: pure, perfect love. The low,
deep male voice then said, "Everything will be alright." Again, I believed him. I was not certain what was going to be alright. But I knew
it would be. After a solid four to five minutes, the music soon faded. I
turned to my husband and began shaking him and yelling. "Jack! Jack!
Wake up!" I am certain I frightened him. I told him of the music and
the voice. He asked me to explain, "What is going to be alright? I didn't
know there was anything wrong." I could not give him an answer that
I didn't know myself. But I also knew the answer would come in time.
All of my worries were suddenly erased, and I felt completely at ease.
With my newfound calm I fell into a deep sleep.

Jack and I did our tour bus trip and nothing eventful happened. On
Monday, June 28, 2004, after returning from our tour bus trip, I sat on
the bedroom floor with suitcases full of dirty clothes. As I sorted them,
I planned the events of the day. Jack was on a trip to Cedar Point
in northern Ohio. I needed to run some errands and get something to
eat because I had absolutely no groceries in the house. Then I remembered that I had a lottery scratch-off ticket worth $10. So I decided I
would cash in the scratch-off ticket when I checked the other
Powerball lottery tickets I had purchased.

First, I took our clothes to the dry cleaners and then headed to a
store at the other end of the shopping center where I could cash in my
ticket. It was almost noon, and I was getting hungry. I walked into the
store, and a young man came over to assist me. He gave me the $10
and began to check the Powerball tickets. I saw a small piece of paper
come up out of the register. The young man looked at me and commented that he had never seen anything like this before. I questioned

him as to what it was. He pulled the paper out of the machine and
proceeded to read it. "Return Powerball ticket to customer. Merchant
unable to pay out of register." Again I questioned him as to what it was
and what it meant. At this point the manager came over. The manager
looked at the paper from the register and then at my Powerball ticket.
He then took another look at the slip of paper and back to my
Powerball ticket. All the while, I had no clue what was going on until
he very calmly told me with a big smile on his face, "My guess is you
just won $100,000."

In disbelief I asked, "Well, how good is your guess?" Leaning over
and handing me the ticket, the manager replied, "99.9 percent." Now
let me state, I very seldom use bad language. I guess I felt it was war-
ranted because out of my mouth spewed, "HOLY SHIT!" I must have
said it rather loud. The other people in the store stopped in their tracks
and turned to look me. But the manager quickly came to my defense
stating, "She just won $100,000." I was so stunned. I burst into tears. I
knew instantly—the voice had been right. Everything would be alright.
And it was. Jack and I listed our condo and sold it within a couple of
months. We were able to buy my mother's home in Columbia City. In
turn, she was able to move into a wonderful senior living facility.

I sometimes lie in bed at night and close my eyes, trying to remember the sound of the singing. I have an ache in my heart to hear it
again. I have yet to succeed, but I know that one day, when it is my
turn to return to the spirit world, I will hear the voices again. I will
hear that low, deep voice speaking to me. I will feel that calm and
peace once again. I will be filled with pure, perfect love. Who knows,
maybe I will be one of the voices singing for someone else here on
earth.

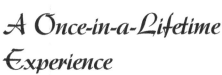

A Once-in-a-Lifetime Experience

Lisa Bunch Letanosky
Tennessee
letanoskylisa@yahoo.com

One night I decided to meditate when all was quiet. No doors were slamming; there was just nothingness around me as my daughter and even the dogs were asleep. If you've never experienced this feeling of nothingness, trust me it's wonderful and you are missing out. Although I was looking forward to this meditative time alone, I had no idea what was about to happen. Aside from my daughter being born, it was the most beautiful, joyous, wonderful experience of my life.

I began to meditate and was on my way to clearing my mind and relaxing when all of a sudden a gush of energy came over me. It felt as though my hair was standing on end. I had my hands clasped together and could feel my fingers, but suddenly my fingers felt very different. It was as though my hands and fingers belonged to someone else. It all felt so weird. I could feel my spirit leaving my body through

185

my head. Although I can't say that I looked down at my body below me, I was definitely aware of it.

The next thing I knew I was seeing colors swirling by, and then I found myself viewing a place—a beautiful one that I had never seen before. It is difficult for me to describe the magnificent beauty that I saw, but I am going to try. The beach was beyond flawless with the water meeting the sand perfectly as though it was a puzzle piecing itself together with every wave that crashed in. The colors were so intensely vivid; it was like nothing I had ever witnessed before.

There were orangy hues so brilliant, so admirable. I remember seeing what looked like a planet or the moon to the left of me just sitting in the water. It was all so close and also made up of an orangy hue with a small amount of light blue. All I can say is the experience far exceeded anything I had ever seen in my life or even ever watched in a movie.

Suddenly there was a light coming towards me; it was bright but not completely white. It was more of a mixture of white with yellow and orange amongst it. Immediately, I knew that this was my father whom I had lost in 1991 and was still grieving. My father and I walked hand in hand along the beach talking and catching up on things though I can't remember the details or what was said. The way I would describe this is that we were more like two lights bound together holding hands.

We talked for what seemed like forever, but yet there was no awareness of time in this place. It is hard for us to understand this on earth as everything we do here is based on the dimension of time. Suffice it to say that there is just no feeling or concept of time there; I can hardly explain it myself.

After our long walk, my father and I flew around in the sky, playing and dancing as if we were two little kids having the time of our lives. We had such a blast, and to this day I can't remember ever having had so much fun and feeling so free. I felt so full of peace and love. When it was time for me to go back, he gently lowered me back down through what appeared to be clouds. I know this seems so stereotypical . . . clouds in heaven . . . but this is exactly what happened.

My father never said goodbye to me; it was more like: *I'll see you later.* All of this communication took place telepathically. We never used our mouths or words to speak. Then I was back in my body.

Getting to visit with my father and unite with him in such a way has made such a big difference in my life. The experience was beyond astonishing and wondrous for me. Because of this, I now never have to wonder if there is life after death. I know there is because I have experienced a piece of heaven for myself. I felt no grief or sorrow afterwards, only love and happiness. Since then I have felt more blessed than anything else.

Admittedly I have tried to meditate and reach my father again, only to be let down. Maybe this was my once in a lifetime experience with him, and I should leave it at that. Once you have had a taste of this beautiful place, why wouldn't you want to go back?

A Close Encounter
of a Heavenly Kind

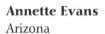

Annette Evans
Arizona

Although I have had a few encounters with angels, this one is most etched in my memory. It brought me to a better understanding with not only myself but also with my Lord and Savior. Yes, angels walk among us, and they come in all shapes, sizes, shades, and ethnicities. Meeting one myself, I came to the realization that they do walk among us and come to us when we need them the most.

I had just turned twenty-five years old and believed at that time in my life that I was ancient. A quarter of a century seemed so depressing. I decided on the chilly winter evening of January 3 that I would pick up a bottle of wine from my local corner store and try to celebrate this very odd number. I didn't want family or friends around and was trying to come to grips with the realization that I wasn't really that old. As I pulled up to the store, there was an old Indian man with khaki clothing sitting near the front door. I stopped and asked him if he needed anything and explained that it was my birthday and that there wasn't any use of a celebration because I was feeling antique. He smiled at me and explained that it was merely the beginning of my life. He said, "God has a plan for you; why not rejoice in your life?" Thinking about it for a few moments, I could not answer. He then looked up at me again with big brown eyes and said, "Why are you wishing to purchase a bottle of wine?" How odd I thought to myself: *How does this man know that I was going to buy wine? How could he have known what I was about to do?*

I continued inside the store, thinking seriously about what he had said. After spending a few minutes browsing the liquor aisle, I decided not to purchase the bottle of wine. Stepping back outside to speak with the gentleman, he had mysteriously disappeared in a matter of minutes. Curious, I proceeded to walk around the building and could not find anyone stirring. Going back inside the minimart, I asked the clerk about the Indian man sitting outside the main entrance. Looking at me oddly, he explained there had not been any Indian man of any ethnicity sitting outside the store. He also stated that he had been working double shifts and that it hadn't been busy all day.

I cordially thanked him, left the store, and got into my car. Since I was a little confused about what had just happened, I trembled as I placed the key into the ignition. As I pulled out of the parking lot, I did not understand that I had just encountered an angel. Finally arriving back home, which was only a couple of miles away, it was at that moment I realized that he was not a human, but in fact an angel sent by God who was delivering a message to me.

My heart leapt with joy, and instead of being depressed and saddened by the funny little number, I was rejoicing and giving thanks for being alive. I spent the rest of my birthday with family and a handful of close friends, celebrating without alcohol.

Although twenty–five seemed like such a depressing age, it turned out to be the best time in my life as it enabled me to create milestones and embrace age in a different light. As each year passes, I find that God has blessed me more and more every day. I thank God to this day for that divine intervention as my special angel gave me understanding at a moment in my life when I needed it most.

Padre Pio: The Mystery of the Stigmata

∙∙∙◄◯◯►∙∙∙

Near us is a celestial spirit, who, from the cradle to the tomb, does not leave us for an instant.   **Padre Pio**

There have been several stigmatics recorded throughout history. The stigmata refer to bodily marks and pain in locations corresponding to the wounds suffered by Jesus Christ during the crucifixion. Reportedly the first instance of the stigmata accepted by the Catholic Church was that of St. Francis of Assisi. Various accounts state that St. Francis had traveled to a Tuscan province in Italy in the celebration of the feast of the Angel Michael and all the other angels. It was there that many say he had a vision of Jesus on the cross and later began to suffer the stigmata. St. Francis died two years later in 1226.

During the following century, the stigmata were also experienced by St. Catherine of Siena. This is not to say that the stigmata had not been suffered by people in more modern times. In fact, one cannot write about this phenomenon without also mentioning Padre Pio of Pietrelcina, a small farming town in Southern Italy.

I must admit here that Padre Pio has personal meaning to me as my parents are from Italy, and I grew up hearing about how wonderful and divine this man was. On September 17, 1915, Padre Pio received his first invisible sign of the stigmata. This is said to occur when one suffers the pain of the wounds endured by Jesus, but however, no visible signs are seen. He did not receive his first visible sign of the stigmata until 1918 when wounds appeared openly on his hands and feet. August 5, 1918 marked the onset of Padre Pio's wound on his side. Although he would bear the wounds of the stigmata for an astounding fifty years, his lesions would never become infected. There was also a fragrant smell that emanated from his wounds during the stigmata. He was evaluated by many physicians who had no logical explanation for what was happening. What is also astonishing is that his wounds reportedly mysteriously disappeared a few minutes after his death.

During his time on this earth, many miracles were and still are being linked to Padre Pio. It is noted, in fact, that more than 1,000 miracles have occurred as a result of Padre Pio's intercession. One such account involves a blind girl named Gemma DiGiorgio who was born without pupils in her eyes. After a visit with Padre Pio, she miraculously regained her sight. The deaf regained their hearing, the sick were cured, and in one noted case a baby was raised from the dead.

As the story goes, a woman was traveling to San Giovanni Rotondo, the home of Padre Pio, to ask the now famous priest to heal her infant son who was very ill. On the way there, the baby died. The mother who was overcome with grief refused to lose faith and continued on her journey. When she reached Padre Pio, she opened a suitcase containing her dead son, screaming in desperation and sorrow. In response, he took the baby in his arms and prayed. After a few minutes, he turned to the mother and said, "Why are you yelling? Don't you see that your child is sleeping?" The mother then looked at the baby to find that he was sleeping peacefully.

In the nineteenth century David Hume, renowned philosopher, economist, and historian, argued that miracles are scientifically impossible because they occur outside the laws of nature. The process of seeking natural explanations for whatever phenomena may occur is known as methodological naturalism.

I find his argument interesting because by definition aren't miracles events which occur outside the laws of nature. So since science works with universal laws, how can science (the natural) explain the supernatural? It's also important to note here that Hume was highly skeptical of God and religion in general. So as a believer, I must make another point. If God does exist and God created this universe, then God must govern its natural laws. And if God governs its natural laws, he must then be able to also suspend them.

Hume also asserts that people should always believe that which is most probable. He argued that no amount of testimony, not even those of eyewitnesses, is enough to prove the existence of a miracle because of the possibility of fraud. It's very hard to support Hume's argument in Padre Pio's case due to the many astounding events that were reported.

Consider the story of a mother who bought her dead baby to Padre Pio. If the baby had just stopped breathing and had then begun breathing again in his presence, you might argue that the baby was never dead but perhaps just unconscious. However, in this case where the baby died and was placed in a suitcase for several hours, how is this possible?

Hundreds of people witnessed the many miracles performed by this now famous friar. In fact, many have claimed to have been healed by praying to him after his death. There are some who say that the wounds of the stigmata are psychosomatic (mentally induced) and others who say they are self-induced or the result of deception.

While some claims have been found to be fraudulent, it is hard to discredit Padre Pio who would often suffer the stigmata in front of church goers and supporters. "Whoever attended just one mass of his, never forgot it," noted a friend of his, Padre Alberto D'Apolito. "It produced such an impression that time and space between the altar and Calvary disappeared. The Mass of Padre Pio visibly reproduced the Passion of Christ, not only in a mystical form, but also physically, in his body. Waves of emotion made Padre Pio tremble at the altar as if the struggle with invisible persons filled him, time and time, with fear, joy, sadness, anguish, and pain. From the expression on his face, one could follow the mysterious dialogue."[7]

---

[7]michaeljournal.org/stpio.htm

Padre Pio was able to read the minds of people, often stating what someone was thinking before one word was ever uttered. He is also said to have been able to see visions of saints, angels, and even the Blessed Mother. It is nearly impossible to note all the mystical experiences attributed to Padre Pio.

A priest named Padre Constantino spoke of a time when he was awestruck by what he saw upon entering the friar's room. "His countenance was shining with a rosy flame of light such as I had never seen before and shall, I think, never see again. It was but for an instant, but I shall never forget it."[8]

A recent survey by the *Pew Forum on Religion* showed that almost 80 percent of Americans believe in miracles. Pope John Paul II canonized Padre Pio making him a saint on June 16, 2002, believed to be one of the greatest miracle workers of all time. More than 300,000 people were said to have attended the canonization ceremony.

Following are two modern-day divine visits attributed to Saint Padre Pio.

---

[8]http://www.spiritdaily.org/pio.htm

Vera's Trip to Italy

---··◦⟨∞⟩◦··---

The following are the words and personal testimony of the late Vera M. Calandra, who passed in August 2004. Vera had promised God that should her dying daughter Vera Marie live, she would help to spread the word about the greatness of Padre Pio, and thus she founded the National Centre for Padre Pio in Barto, Pennsylvania. For more information, please visit <u>www.padrepio.org</u>.

It was in 1963 when a man from my hometown gave my husband and me a book about the life of Padre Pio. But in 1963 my husband had a grocery store, business was good, and the children were coming along fine. Padre Pio was in Italy, and I was in America. And what I'm really trying to say is I had no need for Padre Pio. Isn't it interesting how selfish we are? If we don't have need of someone, well, then, they are just not too important to us. So for all I cared, Padre Pio could stay in Italy.

In 1966 my fifth child was born. Immediately after her delivery the doctor came to my bedside and said, "Mrs. Calandra, your little girl is baptized and is in an ambulance on her way to Children's Hospital in

Philadelphia. There is nothing that can be done for her. She has massive urinary tract defects. She will die within a couple of hours. I was not prepared for those words so I started to cry. I cried louder and louder until finally the sister who had baptized my baby came to me and in a very sweet and gentle voice said, "Please settle down, Mrs. Calandra. Why, this child will be a blessing to you." With the tears coming down my face, I looked at the sister and said, "How could you possibly know how I feel? You're not a mother!" Well, those weren't polite words that I had spoken to the sister.

The author with her family at the National Centre for Padre Pio. With her are her husband John and daughters Erica (far right) and Lia.

I did go back and apologize to her sometime later because hers were kind words of wisdom. The child did become a blessing, not only to me and my family but to thousands and thousands of others. Throughout the world people learned about Padre Pio just because of the illness of that little girl. The little one was still alive the following morning. So the doctor, a very prominent surgeon, looked at her and said, "Surely there is nothing we can do, but we'll open her up and at least hope to make her comfortable. But she'll die very soon now." She was operated on once, twice, three, four times . . . always major surgery, always the same words. Repeatedly the team of surgeons had the same words to speak to us. "We don't know what is keeping this child alive. She is barely hanging on by a thread." We hadn't turned to Padre Pio yet. We were praying to all the popular saints. And with those prayers came promises. They were little ones at first because that was all we were capable of.

Then one day when my little girl was about two years of age, there was nothing more that I could do for her at home. Her fever was raging, and I rushed her back to Children's Hospital. I said, "Doctor, please do something; we don't want this child to die." He said, "Tell me what you want me to do?"

I said, "Well, if you don't do anything, she probably will die, but if you open her up, then maybe there's a chance." He said, "Very well, sign the necessary papers." My husband and I signed them, and we left the hospital that day with very heavy hearts. Surgery was scheduled for very early in the morning. And as we sat at home that evening, we thought: *Will we see her after this? Will she be gone?*

Some relatives and friends came over and said, "Why don't you write to Padre Pio? You know who he is. He's that priest in Italy who they say makes miracles." Well, it was a miracle that I needed now and I needed it very badly. So I went racing through the house to look for the one book that I had read when I didn't need him. I found the book and quickly wrote down the address of the monastery in Italy. There wasn't going to be time for a letter. I would have to send a cable off; I did so.

The child was operated on in the morning. The doctor told us to remain at home until he would call us. It was early afternoon when he called. He said come down; you may see your little one. The doctor told us that she was still alive but in serious condition. Strangely enough, he said, when they had opened her up, her kidneys were not as bad as the x-rays had showed them to be. And those x-rays were taken that very morning before the surgery. However, he said, "We did have to remove her urinary bladder." Well, of course, my heart sank and I said: "But doctor, how can she live without a bladder?" And he said, "She's not going to live."

He had been saying that to us for two years now. I really can't say that my daughter was enjoying life, but she was still alive. I had to hold on. I had to have that hope. Three days later a message came from Padre Pio's monastery. It said, "We send you our blessings. We pray for your intentions and we ask you to pray always to the will of God." Well, the fact that it was a form letter and not at all personal hurt my feelings. He didn't even take the time to write a personal message, but the child was still alive and I thought I should let him know this. So I sent a sent a second cable off to him. Just three days after that second cable, I received a second form letter. I said to my family, "You see, regardless of what you tell them over there, they always tell you the same thing." I wasn't at all impressed with this Padre Pio. I don't even know why I was even praying to him at this time because I didn't believe that he was doing a thing for us. But for one reason or another, I was asking for his help.

About a month and a half later, (August 15, 1968), I was sitting in the living room of my home, and I had a most unusual experience. All around my head was the most beautiful fragrance. It smelled like roses. It startled me. It was so beautiful. I looked from side to side; I had no flowers in the house. Where was this coming from? Then I remembered the one book that I had read about him. It said that if he were praying for your intentions, he could very well send a fragrance. Many who pray to Padre Pio experience this fragrance. I couldn't be sure of it. I had never had this type of experience before. So naturally I questioned it. I said to myself: *Is it possible that this is you, Padre Pio? Well, if it is, I don't understand what you are saying to me. You have to make it clear.* Well, Padre Pio didn't waste any time. He answered right away. He wanted me to bring my little girl to him in Italy. And he said: *Do not delay; come immediately!*

Author's Note: Vera heard Padre Pio speak to her telepathically in her mind.

Then I started to think. I thought of all the promises we made. And as the child was hanging on day by day, the promises were getting bigger and bigger. Right before that last operation, my husband and I prayed, "Dear God, if you allow this child to live, we will do whatever you want us to do." So now he was asking me to come to Italy. How do I manage that? I had never traveled before. I didn't have a passport. I had never been any further than Philadelphia, which was twenty something miles from my home. I didn't know the Italian language. I didn't know where this little monastery was. Not only that what would I do with the new baby (the baby that was born just weeks before this particular date)? I was breastfeeding her as I had done with all the others, and I didn't want to deny her that privilege which would mean that she would have to come with me. How was I going to manage with a very sick child unable to walk in one arm and an infant in the other arm, both completely dependent on me? I didn't know how I was going to manage, but all I knew was Padre Pio said: *Do not delay; come immediately!*

One week later I was standing in the Rome airport, looking around for Padre Pio, but he was nowhere in sight. I was getting very frustrated, standing there by the many, many suitcases, since both children were in diapers. I didn't know how to ask for help, and I didn't know where to go. I was feeling very down. I wanted to get back on that plane, but it was as if a force was pulling me to go on. Like a tremendous magnet, it was pulling me forward. I couldn't stop now; I had to go on. Of course, it was going to be difficult. Look at the big favor I was asking. One day someone said that was faith pulling you. I don't know. I was desperate and I wanted my little girl.

We arrived in San Giovani Rotondo very late that night. The children were very, very cranky. I checked into a hotel. They didn't like the hotel, and they cried and cried. The people in the hotel didn't like the noisy youngsters, and they knocked on our door and they told us so. Early in the morning, I went down to the desk and asked, "Where can I find Padre Pio?" And the man said, "You climb this hill and go up the next hill; turn the corner and you will see the church and the monastery."

I walked into the church and no Padre Pio. I walked into the monastery. I looked around the piazza. I didn't see anyone who looked like Padre Pio. I told the friar standing there, "Father, I'd like to see Padre Pio." You might think that I had told him a joke. His hands went up in the air, and he said, "But everybody in San Giovanni wants to see Padre Pio." I said, "Father, I don't think that's funny. I've come a great distance. My trip was extremely difficult. I have a dying child that the best surgeons in America cannot help. Not only that, I even had to bring the baby. And you know what, Father? I had Padre Pio's perfume; it was so beautiful and so strong; it spoke to me. He called me here, Father, and that's why I came. So tell me, do you think I would have come here at this particular time on my own?" Maybe I convinced Father. He said, "Alright, alright! Come back at 2:30 and you will see Padre Pio."

So 2:30 that afternoon I returned. I was told, "Don't you speak to him unless he speaks to you first." I knelt with my sick child and my infant and I waited. Finally, the door opened and in came Padre Pio.

It was not the middle-aged friar, but instead a very old, but beautiful Padre Pio. He was seated in a wheelchair, and another friar was pushing the wheelchair. He came forward, and he was right in front of us. He put out his hand. He touched the top of the head of my infant and the top of the head of my sick daughter. Then the wheelchair was pushed away. I was unhappy. The friar said, "What's the matter with you?" I said, "Father, is this all? I mean I came from America, and Padre Pio didn't even look at me." He said, "What do you want?" I didn't know what I wanted at this point. He said, "Do you want to see him again," and I said, "Yes, if I may." He then said, "Very well. Come back tomorrow morning at 7:30 and you'll see Padre Pio again."

Well, I searched around in the church a bit, and I discovered the mass schedules and so forth. And I learned when you are in San Giovanni Rotondo, the thing to do was to go to Padre Pio's 5 a.m. mass. So of course that would mean getting up really early. So about 3:30 I jumped out of bed. I had to change diapers, and my sick daughter had many, many surgical dressings that had to be taken care of. I had to get my kids ready and get myself ready. What I'm trying to say is I was late; I was late for his 5 a.m. mass. All those other people, all the lucky ones were sitting way down in the front of the church. The ones who get see him all the time; they were sitting way down in the front of the church. I had to sit in the very last pew and there I sat feeling very sorry for myself. But then again, the mass was over very shortly afterwards.

Well, I wasn't going back to the hotel to wait until 7:30. I decided to go right over to the monastery and wait in the corridor. I had a good hour to kill. While I waited, I had time to think. So I thought about that book, the one book that opened up a new world to me. It said in that book of all the sick who came to Padre Pio, they came from all over the world with every disease imaginable. Not all of them were cured. But we do know they came away stronger just from having been in his presence. The blind who went to Padre Pio, not all had their eyesight restored, but we do know that their vision was improved.

You know what else it said in that book? It said that if you were unable to speak the Italian language, well, then you couldn't make an appointment to confess to Padre Pio. But that wasn't so. It wasn't so

because if you spoke to Padre Pio in whatever language was your language, he could understand you and he could speak to you in that language. And yet he had never studied another language. I thought to myself: *Well, if that's the case, Padre Pio, I'm going to tell you why I'm here and why this little girl,*

Two of the many portraits of Padre Pio found at the Centre.

that the best surgeons in America can do nothing for, is here. And I'm going to tell you about my extremely difficult trip. And I'm going to tell you all of this in English because I can't speak any other language.

At 7:30 the friar came out. He said, "Mrs. Calandra?" I said, "Yes." He said, "You may kneel here in the corridor, and the Padre will come down this way." So I knelt with my sick child and my baby.

The door opens and he is in the same wheelchair and the same friar is pushing the wheel chair. I'm prepared to tell him everything. He's coming closer now, and he's looking into my eyes. And I'm looking into his, but not one single word had passed through these lips. I didn't speak to Padre Pio. I communicated with him through my heart. He was right in front of me. He put out his hand. He put his hand on the top of the infant and again on the top of the head of my sick daugh-

BEATO
PADRE PIO DA PIETRELCINA

ter. I was able to kiss the back of that wounded hand. He extended his hand, and I kissed it. Words spoken not with lips but from a very sincere heart, I said, "Please God, make a miracle so that all the people will believe." I stopped and thought: *I asked for a miracle so that all of you will believe?* But I thought I came here for my child, and yet it didn't even enter my mind. Why did I speak those words? Who's concerned about my child and how we are suffering? And yet I asked for a miracle so that all of you will believe. The next few days were tough. My infant was so sick that I had to take her to the hospital. I couldn't wait until it was time to return to Rome and back to Philadelphia.

When I arrived at Philadelphia airport, what a reception committee there was! Half of my hometown showed up. They all came out to see the hysterical woman who went across the ocean to try to obtain a cure for her child. The questions were flying such as: "Did you see Padre Pio? What was he like? And what did he say to you? What about your little girl? Is she completely cured? And the baby, how did she make out?" What could I answer? What could I really say? Yes, I saw Padre Pio. I wasn't too much impressed with him. He didn't speak a word to me, and I didn't say a word to him—at least not in words. My sick child, take a look at her. I think she's sicker now than when I took her there. Not only that, I even brought the baby home sick. What could I really say?

We were home only a day or so and the hospital called; they wanted x-rays taken of my daughter. This is most unusual. When they sent her home just a couple of months before, they had sent her home to die. Why were they calling now? We didn't know but neither did we question it. We brought her down. The x-rays were taken. It was two whole weeks before they gave us the report, and it was only because we demanded the report at that time. We were told, "There is a remnant of a bladder present in the x-ray." Now, as I had mentioned, the doctors had removed her urinary bladder before we went to Padre Pio. I asked, "Do you think it might grow?" And he said, "If it does, I'll be sure to write a book about her."

Three days later Padre Pio died. I knew then what a very special grace had been given us. I had the strength and the courage to make that extremely difficult trip across the ocean to a foreign land, not knowing where I was going or what would be the end result because

I was desperate. Had I not gone, I don't know what would have happened to my daughter. But then again, I don't have to worry about that. The doctor said, "Come back in six months." We went back to Children's Hospital, and at that time he confirmed, "Your daughter has a new bladder." I said, "Doctor, can you explain this?" and he said, "Hardly. When an organ is removed from the body through an accident or through surgery, it doesn't grow again. It doesn't regenerate." My husband didn't care how busy he was in the grocery store. The following year in 1969 we went to Padre Pio's tomb in Italy to kneel in thanks for the very special grace that he obtained for us. The little one started to get better day by day. She was able to eat; she was able to walk. You could see the new life growing in her.

A Miracle at Christmas

————••◇•◇>••————

Cindy Griffith–Bennett
New York
www.psychicsupport.com

AUTHOR'S NOTE: The full version of this story appears in *Voyage of Purpose* by David Bennett and Cindy-Griffith Bennett, published by Findhorn Press, 2011.

On a snowy Christmas Day 2000, we were blessed by a miraculous visit from a true Christmas angel. We now know that miracles do happen and that if you are open to receiving, they can come at any time. Let me give you a little background, so you can understand the blessing we received that day.

My husband Dave had recently been diagnosed with Stage 4 lung and bone cancer. At the time the doctors said he had only weeks left. We were trying to stay positive, looking at an optimistic ten-year plan while at the same time taking care of his affairs. Since radiation and chemotherapy treatments deplete white blood cells that help to fight off infection, my husband wouldn't have been able to fight off an infection if he had gotten sick. Thus we decided that Christmas with the family that year was not in our best interest, so I made plans to visit with my family the day after Christmas instead. This was the first Christmas that I had missed in my thirty-nine years!

Family guilt, self-inflicted or not, is one of the worst types. I called a number of times throughout the day, and with all the "We miss you!" and "We are running behind schedule, you always keep us on track!" the guilt kept piling on! About 5 p.m. on Christmas Day, the phone rang. I typically have a lot of clients calling for appointments, so on days I am not working, I usually screen my calls. For some unknown reason, this time I just automatically picked up the phone.

"Hi, Cindy," said the unidentified voice. As she kept talking, I recognized the English accent as this very sweet massage therapist that specializes in Thai Massage. "Have you ever heard of Padre Pio?" I told her that I had visited Padre Pio's monastery when I had made a trip to Italy. He lived until the 1960s. Padre Pio was known for his compassion and healing works. He was also known to bilocate (be in two places at once). It is documented that during the Second World War the air force was going to accidentally bomb an area that was occupied by Allies. The fighter pilots reported a monk appearing in the air in front of the plane, motioning for them to go back. They were so scared that they did go back, and the disaster was averted!

This woman then asked if I had heard about the healing miracles that happened around a glove of Padre Pio's. This I was unaware of. She offered to put another woman on the phone to tell me about it.

The woman had a very sweet and calming voice. As it turned out, she was a local television personality Nancy Duffy, known for her beauty inside and out. She started to tell me about Padre Pio's glove. A priest who had been a custodian of Padre Pio in Italy had returned to his parish in Brooklyn, New York, with two of the gloves that Padre Pio had worn to cover his wounds. These gloves were considered sacred and known to have healing properties. There were multiple stories of how the glove healed the parishioners of this Brooklyn church. One thing that helps support this claim is the uncanny and beautiful rose scent that emanates from the glove. It grows stronger and weaker, yet is always present.

Nancy told me that the priest kept one glove for himself and gave one to his sister. The sister felt that it really should be available for all to benefit from. She figured that the parking lot attendant knew everyone from the parish, so he would be the best guardian for the glove. The glove shares a box with a sheet that came from Padre Pio's bed, a book that people write to Padre Pio in, and one of those famous double image pictures of Padre Pio that changes as you tilt the picture from side to side. The attendant gives the box to whoever needs it. There was a waiting list which the woman on the other end of the phone had somehow gotten on, and so on Christmas Eve she had received the glove for two days. Our English friend had told her about Dave's cancer, and she had called to see if Dave would like to touch the miraculous glove.

My husband was tired from a visit earlier in the day, and when I mentioned this, the woman kindly offered to come to us. For those of you that don't know where we live, it is known as Windy Hill. Our place used to be a cross country ski resort on top of a high hill that is often buffeted with lake-effect snow. We were currently getting hit with a snowstorm. The landlord was out of town so the drive hadn't been plowed. This stranger was still willing to make the trip! We gave her directions, and an hour and a half later, via cell phones, we guided her into our hard-to-find driveway.

She arrived, covered with snow and bearing a canvas tote. We sat in our living room, and she pulled out a wooden box with a little picture of Padre Pio on the top. She gently opened it and took out the picture, a little book, and then gently brought out the glove. At first I was surprised. It was a tiny brown glove with no fingers in it. It looked like a glove you would see on a homeless person.

The little brown glove had a simple metal cross gently sown onto the top side. Later, when I turned it over, I saw that someone had sown a tiny piece of cloth with a little cross in the place that must have been where the hand wound from the stigmata was. The amazing thing to us was the aroma that came from it. Anyone who smelled this rose scent could tell you that it's like no other rose smell you had ever smelled. You couldn't recreate it even with the best of oils or perfume. The sheet from his bed also had that scent. The sheet was in a little plastic bag, but the glove was not.

Dave put the glove in his hand, and you could just feel the calm that came over him. This is how he explained it to me, "At first, I just sensed a type of love similar to what I had felt when I had my near-death experience. When I touched the glove, I was feeling with my heart and not my mind. I could feel my heart opening up to feel that light and love. I could feel both spirit and human emotion because it was vast amounts of unconditional love. It is similar to going back into the light a little bit, but not all the way. In order to experience the near death, you have to accept that light back. I have been having trouble keeping my heart open and working with my light and love because of the physical fatigue and drug-induced emotions. But as I stroked the glove, it felt like some of the barriers were just melting away and the light in my heart was just able to open and shine as bright as ever. Well, I could just say that my spirit was singing. Spirit gets in this joyous frame of (not mind but) spirit. When spirit is joyous, it feels like a song in your heart, and it interacts with your human emotions. It just brings tears to the corners of the eyes. It gets you a little choked up. You can feel it emanate throughout your whole body. It isn't just your heart that expands; it expands your entire body physically."

As our new friend told Dave the glove's story and how she had ended up with it, he sat and stroked the sacred glove as it lay in his right hand. Later he told me he could actually feel the glove, which is its own little miracle as he has permanent nerve damage in that hand and hadn't felt any sensation with it for over six months!

He handed me the glove, and I could immediately feel the energy coming from the center of it. I felt calm and at peace. I knew this was real. I handed it back to Dave and then took the piece of sheet from the little bag. Again I was taken aback by the indescribably intense rose scent growing in the room as she and Dave talked about everything from his near-death experience to the wonderful experiences she had had while the glove was in her possession. She said she felt like a Christmas angel. We told her that she was definitely our Christmas angel! The rose scent kept growing stronger and stronger and was starting to fill the room. It was accompanied by a pervading sense of peace and love.

At one point our Christmas angel stopped the conversation and said, "I have had this glove for two days and the rose scent has grown stronger and weaker depending on who was holding it, but I have never smelled it this strong!" She was amazed. The smell had filled the whole house by now and so had the sense of peace and love. Together we shared stories, feelings, hot tea, and gingerbread cookies as if we were old friends. An hour and half later, our Christmas angel was calling the next person she was going to share the glove with to let him know she was on her way! We wondered if she had been able to spend any holiday time with her family, and due to the number of people she had visited, we doubted that she had.

Later when we went to bed, Dave told me that he could still smell the roses. I couldn't smell them, yet the minute I reached over to touch his hand and made contact, I could smell the roses too! I slept through the rest of the miracle, but here is how Dave explained it to me the next day. "I could smell the roses as we went to bed. It just made me go into a really nice, calm, peaceful sleep. It helped my body to relax and drift off to sleep which is a lot closer to normal than what I have experienced in a long time. I don't just drop off to sleep that easily lately. I used to be able to just go to sleep right away; now I have to sit. That night I went right to sleep, and it reminded me of when we used to do a nice pipe ceremony (A Native American tradition of giving thanks and offering prayer). It was very comforting. The smell of the roses and the glove just comforted me. I was able to get a restful sleep."

He continued, "At two o'clock I awoke and the smell of roses was just as it was everywhere. I just started to cry. I could feel my heart open fully, and I could feel my light and my spirit shining as bright as in my near death. So, I got up, meditated, and just enjoyed taking that energy in."

Angels don't always have wings; sometimes they appear in a snow-covered coat and a scarf. The next day I was telling one of my clients about our Christmas miracle. She was instantly reminded that someone had given her a medallion of Padre Pio's about three months earlier for her daughter who has neurological impairments. She said that she had been carrying this medallion around in her purse and never thought to have her daughter hold it the way Dave had held the glove. She asked me to hold on while she went and got the medallion. She hadn't taken it out of the box. I felt as if I was getting to experience the blessing of the night before all over again!

She came back to the phone and sounded like she was in shock. She had opened the case and what she smelled causes shivers to run up and down both our spine. Roses, she smelled roses. Her daughter was being fussy in the background, and my client decided to put the medallion in her daughter's hand. Instantly the girl calmed down and started her version of talking. My client and I sat, in two different states, in silence. I felt like the Christmas miracle was being passed on. My client told me that she had realized as she was getting the medallion out of her purse that it must go back to the woman who originally gave the medallion to her. It turns out that the woman had been diagnosed with cancer. My client realized that the medallion didn't need to be hoarded; it needed to be shared. She was going to return the medallion in the next few days. The miracle was being passed on.

As for my husband, Dave has been in remission since April of 2001. The doctors didn't believe it at first, but he is still in remission and doing well. We feel very blessed by both God and Padre Pio. Miracles are very real; we received one that Christmas Day 2000. The glove is no longer at that church and we do not know how to get a hold of it, but you can get the medallions through the Padre Pio Foundation.

A Ray of Hope

---··◄◯►··---

Be thou the rainbow in the storms of life. The evening beam that smiles the clouds away, and tints tomorrow with prophetic ray.

Lord Byron

Have you ever gone through the various stages of your life and wondered why certain strangers entered it at the most opportune time? These are the people that you feel an unexplainable connection to for no apparent reason. Perhaps you've pondered what your life would have been like had these chance encounters not taken place at all. Or maybe you believe that these encounters were not by chance but in fact part of some divine plan.

If I were to ponder all the different stages of my life, I couldn't help but think of an incredible man named Ray Skop. A friend had told me about a faith healer in Jersey City who had helped her husband beat cancer. She had offered to take me to see him, but we never got around to it. Then a few years later while I was doing research for this book, I happened to come across a Web site for the Ray of Hope Foundation,

211

a nonprofit organization founded in order to help children in need. The Web site contains testimonials by people who say they were cured with Ray's help. The more I read about this man, the more I wanted to meet him. After making contact via email with a woman listed on his Web site named Anne DuHaime, a meeting was arranged. We went back and forth with dates that were convenient for both of us and finally settled on Monday, December 12, 2011. Although I did not know it at the time, this date was very noteworthy. But before I explain the significance behind this date, I want to introduce you to a beautiful girl named Sammi (Samantha Rose) who also happens to be Anne's granddaughter.

In 1999 Sammi was an active two-year-old with beautiful curly hair and a contagious smile that would warm the hearts of all who saw her. She loved to run and play and do all the things typical of most toddlers her age until the day came when, for no apparent reason, she could no longer walk. Her parents, Deeni and Mark Saltarelli, took her to several doctors and specialists; however, no one could find the cause of their daughter's sudden lack of strength and partial paralysis.

Sammi's fate changed when the family pediatrician told her mother about Ray, a man he said many people claimed performed miracles. Her mom tried repeatedly to reach Ray and finally got a hold of him on November 30, which also happened to be her deceased grandmother's birthday—a woman, she said, who was very religious and also prayed the rosary. When Ray answered the phone, he surprised her by saying that he was expecting her phone call. "I've been waiting for you to call," he told her. "Your daughter will be fine." Ray invited both Sammi and her mother to his home where a large crowd had gathered outside. Despite the fact that it was a brisk day on December 3, a rose bush stood in front of the house remarkably in full bloom.

Once inside his home, Ray along with members of his rosary group prayed for Sammi. He then explained to Deeni that he knew she was coming because angels had appeared to him in the sky. He had also had a dream about this beautiful little girl so he already knew that everything was going to be okay. In fact, on December 7 he called Deeni and confidently went on to tell her not to worry because her little daughter would walk by that upcoming weekend if she would only promise to say the rosary once a week for the rest of her life.

Deeni, of course, agreed without hesitation.

The following day, December 8, Sammi was taken to Columbia Hospital in New York where she was examined by seven different neurologists. However, her parents later went home yet again with no official diagnosis. There were still no answers. December 8 marks the Feast of the Immaculate Conception which

Deeni Saltarelli with her daughter, Sammi

celebrates the immaculate conception of the Virgin Mary. The following Saturday morning, December 11, Sammi began to show some improvement as she was finally able to put her legs and feet down properly (her feet had been bending backwards from lack of use). At the same time her mother was witnessing this, the phone rang. It was Ray. "You must believe," he told her, "I promise you she will walk by this weekend."

Later that night, her legs turned red from her knees down, and by the next morning she woke up telling her parents that she wanted to walk. Although she fell down at first, she just got up and tried again. It was December 12, which is the feast of Our Lady of Guadalupe. Sammi was completely healed, and once again running and walking all over the place to the shock and delight of both her family and her physicians.

The story of Our Lady of Guadalupe goes back to the sixteenth century when a man named Juan Diego from a small village near Mexico City was on his way to mass in honor of the Blessed Mother. Suddenly, the story goes, Mary appeared dressed like an Aztec princess and told Juan Diego to tell the bishop of Mexico to build a chapel in that spot.

He did as he was told, but the bishop asked for proof. At the same time Juan Diego's uncle became ill, and Our Lady appeared to him again assuring him that his uncle would be fine. She also gave Juan Diego roses to bring to the bishop in his tilma or cape. When Juan Diego later opened his tilma before the bishop, the roses fell to the ground and an image of Mary appeared, bringing the bishop to his knees. The day was December 12, 1531.

It is also interesting to note that a total of forty days had passed from the time Sammi stopped walking to the day that she was healed. Forty is a very significant and symbolic number in the Bible. The season of Lent lasts for forty days, representing Jesus' time fasting and resisting temptation from Satan in the dessert. Noah also watched rain fall and Moses was on Sinai waiting for the Ten Commandments, both for forty days. Another interesting point is that a woman carries a baby for forty weeks. So was it just a coincidence that Sammi's ordeal lasted for exactly forty days? Her mom certainly doesn't think so. And was it a coincidence that I happened to meet Ray on the twelfth anniversary of Sammi's miraculous healing and the feast of Our Lady of Guadalupe? I don't think so. As I've said earlier in this book, I don't believe in coincidences. There are only "Godincidences." Everything happens for a reason.

This was one of those days that I will remember forever. I was nervous about meeting this so-called miracle worker from Jersey City, and I'll admit I was a bit skeptical. Yet I swiftly realized that I had nothing to be anxious about. Ray quickly put me at ease with his calming and reassuring demeanor. As I interviewed him, I felt an unexplainable yet unmistakable connection to him. I clearly felt that our meeting was not by chance.

Ray and I met at his Rosary House on Hawthorne Avenue in Jersey City. People from all over the country have come there to meet Ray and pray with him. As I sat there facing him that day, I couldn't help but notice a beautiful tin painting behind him. This painting, known as the Weeping Madonna to many, depicts Mary (around age ten) with her mother St. Anne. Many years ago as a young teen, Ray happened to see the painting on the curb in front of an old house in town and rescued it from the garbage as a gift for his mother.

In 1998 the painting resurfaced in his parent's garage covered with oil. Again, he decided to rescue the painting and clean it up. Two days later, however, the painting began to exude new oil. He tried cleaning it again, but it was no use for the oil would continue to appear. Ray was baffled and showed the painting to several friends and family members. One family member told him that the Blessed Mother was

Ray's picture of the Weeping Madonna

calling him and that he needed to say the rosary. He listened and his life hasn't been the same since.

He began to have many unexplainable metaphysical experiences. To name a few, religious statues in his bedroom appeared to move; Arabic symbols appeared on the walls, and a rose bush in front on his home continued to bloom during the cold months of winter. It is interesting to note here that Ray's home is on Hawthorne Avenue in the Marian section of Jersey City in the same spot where the Blessed Mother reportedly appeared more than seventy-five years ago.

(Supernatural events in which the Blessed Mother was believed to appear are known as Marian apparitions). Also the crown of Jesus was made from a Hawthorne bush.

If you ask him what religious experience has impacted him the most, he will quickly tell you about an

Ray Skop and his stigmata

unforgettable, traumatic event which took place on Good Friday during Holy Week in 1999 when he suddenly noticed his palms bleeding. "When it first began, my palms, forehead, feet, and side became itchy. I first noticed blood coming from the palms of my hands and thought I had scraped them. Then I also noticed blood on my socks and on my side. I was very frightened and didn't know what to think at first," he explained. Ray then sought the help of a local priest who immediately began to kneel in prayer upon witnessing the bleeding, sensing that this humble man was actually experiencing the stigmata. St. Francis of Assisi and Padre Pio are also known for experiencing this phenomenon in which the subjects bleed in the same areas that Jesus was tortured during the crucifixion.

Interestingly, Ray is a diabetic and has to check his blood sugar levels often. During one of his experiences, the blood was tested from his stigmata and no sugar was found. At the same time his blood from another area of his body was tested and sugar was indeed found! Doctors have no explanation for this phenomenon.

Since then the bleedings occur sporadically and most often on church feast days, especially Good Friday. Ray noted that he feels tremendous pressure on his hands as though something is being forced through them. When asked about his comparison to Padre Pio, he takes it all in stride and refuses to take credit for any of the miracles which have been attributed to him saying, "It's all up to the man upstairs. I get this feeling that comes over me and I know whether or not I can help someone."

In addition to Sammi, whom I mentioned earlier, Ray has been credited with many other miracles. On the following pages I will note several of these incredulous events in the very words of those who experienced them. I begin with a beautiful story which tells of a love between mother and son which could not be broken.

I'm Bringing You Back

June Taglianetti
Kristopher Taglianetti
New Jersey
Rottie465@aol.com

After being found comatose and unresponsive on March 13, 2011, my son Kris, then thirty-four years of age, was rushed to the hospital by ambulance. His condition was so dire that it took the EMS workers nearly two hours just to stabilize him. When doctors finally examined him at the hospital, they believed Kris would die within five hours.

Although thankfully he did make it through the night, his condition did not improve. My son had undetected pneumonia leading to Rhabdomyolysis which is the breakdown of muscles in the body. When this happens, damaged cells and poison get into the bloodstream, and the body begins to shut down. Kris ended up having three strokes and was on dialysis two times a day. It was a mother's worst nightmare come true when on the third day a neurologist took a CT scan and told me and my family that this was the best we could hope for. He bluntly told us that Kris had no brain waves and was dying rapidly. We asked if things could possibly improve and were told, "No, this is the best it could get."

This same doctor encouraged us to unplug all life support and let him die. If I had not witnessed this conversation, I would not have believed it.

Maybe it was denial or maybe it was mother's intuition, I don't know, but I re-

Ray Skop is pictured here at his Rosary House with Kris Taglianetti. Notice the orbs in the photo. Orbs are how spirit energy often manifests in photographs.

fused to give up hope and kept telling my son, who was still unconscious, to keep fighting. Later that day a friend suggested that we contact a healer named Ray from Jersey City. We immediately agreed, and it was arranged for Ray to call my husband's cell phone that evening. We got special permission by hospital personnel to use the cell phone next to the machines. When Ray called, my husband put the receiver on speaker phone so everyone in the room could hear what was going on. The following is Ray's account of what happened:

"It's not me that does the helping," explained Ray. "It is Mother Mary, Jesus, or Saint Anne. I explained to Kris' father that I couldn't promise anything but told him to put the phone next to his son's ear. When he did, a feeling came over me, and I knew that I could help Kris. So I began to talk to Kris saying, 'Kristopher, my name is Ray. Your father has come to me to help you. Your whole family has come to me to help you.

'You've crossed over to the Other Side but don't belong there. Do you see the beautiful lake that you are standing by? You're on the

Other Side, and I'm on this side. This place is truly beautiful. Kristopher, take my hand. I'm bringing you back. Don't be afraid. You have to trust me. I'm bringing you back. Don't look back at the light. Just keep looking forward and stop being fidgety and nervous. Just come with me. You're back. Now, you will start to breathe and you will begin life again as you knew it."

Miraculously later that night, Kris began waving to the nurses. When I questioned the doctors and nurses, I was told that it was just a reflex and that my son's situation was grim. Well, the situation may have been grim, but Kris did survive. In fact, he continued to beat the odds from that very same night Ray spoke to him. The next morning his oxygen levels incredulously shot way up and the doctors removed the breathing tube. Although Kris immediately began breathing on his own, we were told that he had brain damage. But again they were wrong. He had no brain damage whatsoever.

Next they told us that Kris would surely be confined to a wheelchair. Again they were wrong. Although he spent a long time recovering in rehab, he is now walking on his own. We were also told that my son's kidneys were in bad shape and might never recover. Today his kidneys are perfectly normal.

Throughout this whole ordeal, I never gave up on my son. I prayed and had faith that everything was going to be alright. And I thank God for sending me an angel who took my side. I have no doubt that Ray, Jesus, the Blessed Mother, and others brought my son back his health and his life. Truthfully I was never really a religious person, but now I believe so strongly in the power of prayer and know that I have been blessed with a divine intervention.

Ray is more than a "ray of hope." He literally performs miracles. My son is living proof.

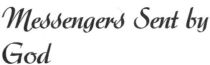

Messengers Sent by God

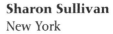

Sharon Sullivan
New York

In the midst of our many challenges in life, angels do visit us. We are thankful to Ray Skop and his Ray of Hope Prayer Group for being such angels and for also being instrumental in inviting others into our lives to help us during our time of trial.

On Tuesday, June 14, 2005, my husband Tom began to feel very ill. He first attributed it to working outside in the heat and decided to come home early to rest and drink fluids. Although Tom thought doing so would help, it did not. The next day he went to see his doctor who maintained it was probably due to the heat. Rest and fluids were prescribed. By this time, however, Tom was also experiencing in both feet tingling pain ascending up into his legs and flu-like pain throughout the body. When evening brought no relief, we went to the ER. IV fluids were administered, and he was sent home.

On Thursday there was no improvement. Although Tom did try to go to work, he could hardly function. The girls in his office called me, saying that they were very worried about him. He's quite a trooper in the face of adversity, but his strength was severely flagging. He went back to the doctor, and this time he saw his physician's partner who ordered additional tests that resulted in no diagnosis. We then revisited the emergency room that evening. More tests showed nothing, and things were slowly getting worse.

Friday morning, in a leap of faith, we proceeded with our plans to close on our new home a hundred miles away. When Tom tried to get out of the car for the walk through, he couldn't walk. His legs were weak and seemingly paralyzed. At the closing, the realtor and I supported him, escorting him into the room. By then, his hands were so numb and painful; he could hardly sign the paperwork. After the closing, we drove immediately back to New Jersey for the third visit to the ER.

Finding the ER packed, with Tom paralyzed and in extreme pain, we realized we had a long wait ahead of us. Suddenly a familiar voice asked us what was wrong. Tom's cousin, an ER nurse, was on duty that night. She quickly expedited Tom's care and vouched for the fact that it "wasn't all in his head!" Tom was finally admitted to the hospital for observation, not knowing what was wrong.

We contacted family and friends to let them know Tom was in the hospital and that we needed everyone's prayers. Anne DuHaime, the wife of Tom's cousin, was among those told of Tom's condition. She immediately contacted her daughter, who had already experienced the healing powers of the oils in their lives. Debbie DuHaime called Tom, and Ray Skop prayed with Tom over the phone. Tom was now under the care of a skillful neurologist and in the hands of God via the prayers of Ray and his prayer group plus many other friends and family.

After many, often, painful tests, the diagnosis came down as Guillain-Barré syndrome (GBS), a rare autoimmune condition affecting only about one per 100,000, in which the body's immune system attacks the body's own nerves causing increasing pain and paralysis. My husband underwent five days of intense treatment with gamma globulin. The oils from Ray Skop arrived on Monday. We began to administer the oils right away. A dear friend also came to visit, praying

over Tom and using the healing of Reiki on him. In faith we jour-
neyed, trusting that we were doing all in our power and leaving the
rest to God.

That was when it began—the unforeseen intervention of people
whom I can only describe as "angels." One afternoon in the hospital as
I chatted with a woman who was visiting her elderly mother, a patient's
voice cried out from across the hall, "Jesus loves you!" The woman, a
born-again Christian, was quick to identify this as a message for me.
The next day as I was passing along the street in my town, a total
stranger stopped me to say, "Do you know Jesus loves you?" I told her
that I had recently been assured of this!

After several days Tom was moved to a rehab center (a.k.a. nursing
home). He was suffering both physical and mental anguish, not knowing what the outcome of all this would be. On the way to visit him, I
had stopped at a Dunkin' Donuts. Once there I called Tom to see if he
wanted me to bring him some coffee. Suddenly an older man sitting in
the corner asked me what I was doing. I explained briefly and told
him he probably wouldn't understand my concerns as the majority of
people have never heard of this "disease" my husband had, namely
Guillain-Barré. "Actually," he answered, "I understand it quite well. I
am a doctor who has treated many with this condition. Your husband
will get well." As if this good news and confident assurance were not
enough, the man looked up and began to pray for my husband, **out
loud**, right there in Dunkin' Donuts.

Now I ask you, did all these people come coincidentally into our
lives or were they messengers sent by God to give us strength and
courage? I can only say that such things have never before happened
nor have they since. Tom did eventually recover, and we do believe his
physical healing was a miracle, attributed to both prayer and modern
medicine. There is no doubt in my mind, however, that God spoke to
us through many people, some strangers, who could have been none
other than angels.

Miracle Babies

---···◆⟨∞⟩◆···---

Shayna Adee
New York

For more than five years, my husband and I tried unsuccessfully to have a baby. At thirty-eight I had gone to over thirty health care professionals, both allopathic and naturopathic. Many were considered to be at the top of their fields. During this time I tried every modality under the sun with an out-of-pocket expense of thousands of dollars. Everything from holistic health programs and yoga to acupuncture were explored; I even had my amalgam dental fillings replaced. Nothing worked so I finally decided to try in vitro fertilization (IVF). I was under the care of one of the most renowned IVF doctors in the country, but after just one round of treatment and a careful review of my lab results, he informed me that I had only a 20 percent chance of having a baby.

In his opinion my eggs were just too old, and he felt I should consider either an egg donor or adoption. All this was, of course, very upsetting to me and my husband Patrick. One night when Patrick was on a business trip, I was home alone in a new house we had just purchased in a very rural area. After the third devastating miscarriage, we needed a change of scenery.

So on this night, I had time to really reflect on my life and was finally at the end of my rope. I cried out to God shouting, "Please show me a sign; I won't be afraid even if I see an angel. I need to know what you want me to do! Is it your will that I have children or not? I will be okay, but I just need to know. I can't take this anymore!"

Shayna Adee pictured with Ray Skop and her family

Two days later on Thursday, February 12, 2004, I called yet another holistic health center. While making my appointment, I described my situation to one of the health practitioners who surprised me by first asking if I was a spiritual person. In response I was honest and told her that although I was, my faith had been very low lately. She then proceeded to tell me about a healer named Ray in Jersey City and gave me a number to reach him. I did call and talked to a woman named Deeni who was very optimistic as she listened to my story. She later gave the message to Ray, and he called me the next day with Denni on another line. Together we prayed to Jesus, St. Anne, and the Blessed Mother.

About an hour later I noticed a strange heat on the center of my forehead. It was so profound that I even told my husband about it. Although I didn't realize it at the time, this is actually the area where the pituitary gland is located and this gland regulates our hormones.

My husband and I then visited with Ray, his wife Nancy, Deeni, and another woman named Debbie at his Rosary House the following week. They told me about his weeping paintings and statues and then gave me two packets containing the mysterious oil. Every night I would take some of this oil and place it on the area where my ovaries are located and pray. I would also say the rosaries daily.

One day I told a man at work named Frank about my meeting with Ray, and he asked me for a packet of the oil. His wife, he said, had been suffering from terrible neck pain for years. I knew I had only two packets at home, but miraculously when I went to get my keys out of my purse that day, an extra packet showed up. Shocked, I gave it to Frank. Two weeks later his wife's neck was healed.

Every Sunday Ray, Deeni, and Debbie would go out of their way to call me and my husband to pray over the phone. Through those calls I learned more about Ray's incredible gift. I told him about how I asked God to see an angel. Ray told me that he is considered the messenger, which means angel in Greek. I also told him about the heat on my forehead after our first prayer session and was told that it is actually common to experience intense heat in an area of healing.

Ray prayed for me to get pregnant and for the baby to be born on December 8, the feast of The Immaculate Conception. In May I was ecstatic when I found out I was pregnant. My due date was none other than December 8! I gave birth to a beautiful baby girl a few days after my due date and we named her Gabriella Noel—after the angel Gabriel.

Three years later, almost to the day that I learned about Ray, Alana Joelle was born. Then in 2009 I had my third baby girl, Juliana Colette on October 23—eight years to the exact day of my last miscarriage! So as you can see, all three birthdates were symbolic in some way.

Going through infertility was certainly one of the most difficult challenges in my life. But these days as I look at the bigger picture, it also turned out to be one of the biggest blessings in my life. I not only have three beautiful, healthy kids but also have a stronger relation-ship with Jesus. In the end I learned how to have faith. As in Hebrews 11:1 (NIV): "Now faith is confidence in what we hope for and assur-ance about what we do not see."

A Cure for Cancer

Margaret
New Jersey

After the birth of my fourth child, I began experiencing back pain. At first I thought it was just an aftereffect of my labor, but when the pain continued, I went to see a doctor. At first he thought it was just a kidney infection and was going to send me home with antibiotics. But when he sent me for a CT scan just to be safe, the results showed that I had enlarged lymph nodes. Further testing revealed a terrifying diagnosis—it was non-Hodgkin's lymphoma for which there is no cure.

My husband and I were shocked. Here we were with four young children ages 6, 4, 2, and newborn who were faced with the possibility of losing their mother. A bone marrow test further revealed that the cancer had spread to my bones. And to make matters even worse, after going for a second opinion, my husband was told to make funeral arrangements for me for I was in Stage 4 and there was no hope.

Since there is no cure, my doctors told me that my only hope was

229

to slow it down with chemotherapy. At the same time all this was going on, my mother was battling breast cancer and died shortly after. Then after already completing two rounds chemo treatments, a woman named Mary told me about Ray whom she said suffered the stigmata. This man she told us apparently was able to cure people and perform miracles.

My husband and I figured we had nothing to lose at that point, and we went to see Ray. After telling Ray about my diagnosis, we all knelt down and prayed. It is important to note here that although my husband is Catholic and was baptized, I was not. Mary took me to see Father John, who was Ray's friend. Because my situation was deemed an emergency, Fr. John was allowed to baptize me and then give me both my communion and confirmation. Mary suddenly became my godmother.

That same night after closing my eyes, I saw a vision of the Blessed Mother. Although she did not speak, she smiled and we shared a connection that I cannot explain. I simply understood that everything was going to be okay and that I would be healed.

Also on this unforgettable night, I experienced a strange numbness in my body as I lay in bed. The numbness continued for an additional three nights. Somehow I knew that this was a sign of my healing, but I was afraid to say something to the doctor. I figured he'd think I was crazy if I told him to order another CT scan.

But then I met a perfect stranger who blessed me out of the blue and assured me that I was healed. At the same time I couldn't shake off this strong feeling that my mother's spirit was present, telling me that I needed to be rechecked. So I finally worked up enough nerve to call the doctor. But he wouldn't agree to give me the CT scan until I adamantly told him that I would refuse chemo unless he ordered the test and only then did my doctor reluctantly agree.

Shockingly the results revealed no signs of cancer. My oncologist was absolutely stunned, telling me, "It couldn't have been because of the chemo." Although we both knew that a miracle had taken place, my doctor wanted me to continue with my chemo treatments to "be on the safe side."

At first I listened to the doctor and continued with my treatments, but then I became so ill that I refused to do it anymore. In my heart I knew that I was already healed—the Blessed Mother had told me so. After informing my doctor that I would no longer take chemo, I promised him that I would get a CT scan every six months to make sure that the cancer did not return. Today, more than eleven years later, I am still cancer-free. Since that day there have been no further signs of cancer.

These days I feel completely blessed, and my life hasn't been the same since. I know that God is continuing to watch over me, and I have, in fact, been given proof. For one, I was blessed with another healthy baby. Then one day as I looked up into the clouds, I clearly saw the words "Jesus lives." On yet another day as I was driving behind a truck, I saw a beautiful picture of Jesus. But when I drove closer to the truck, there was no picture.

Looking back, I don't know why God has blessed me in so many ways. But I do know that miracles do happen and that God has helpers on this earth. One of them is named Ray.

A Lump on My Breast

Annette Bianchi
New Jersey

Three days before a family vacation to Italy, I discovered a lump on my right breast and immediately went to my ob-gyn. He checked each breast, found the lump, and told me to see his highly recommended oncologist as soon as possible.

Since my upcoming trip to Italy was so important to my family both here and abroad, I didn't want to disappoint everyone with my bad news. I asked my doctor if the oncology appointment could wait for three weeks until I returned from Italy. He himself made the phone call and scheduled my appointment with the oncologist the day after I returned from my trip.

After swearing her to secrecy, the only person I told was my sister Marie who in turn told our mutual friend Liz. Our friend is very spiritual and has always had a deep faith in God. Liz is one of six women who founded a rosary group called the Westlake Rosarians and also attends another rosary group in Northern New Jersey called the "Ray of Hope." Ray is known to suffer the stigmata and owns several religious pictures and statues that "cry" oil. Liz believed that this oil could help me in my time of need and gave some to my sister to give to me.

Things went as planned and I left for my trip to Italy, but each and every day I secretly took an oiled cotton ball and touched my right breast with it as I prayed silently and privately to Jesus and the Blessed Mother that their will be done. Our trip was absolutely wonderful, and a very special bond was formed between our Italian and American families.

When I finally arrived home, I was very nervous about my visit to the oncologist the next day. I was so nervous in fact that I arrived at 10 a.m. even though my scheduled appointment was not until 11:30 a.m. During a very long, thorough exam, the doctor poked and prodded until my breasts literally hurt. After several minutes surveying my x-rays, she asked me which breast the lump was originally found in. She then explained that she could find no sign of any lump in either breast. Of course, I was very happy to hear this, but I couldn't help but wonder if this was good news or rather a case of a very bad doctor.

I left the oncologist's office and went straight to my ob–gyn's office. Again, my breasts were examined, and lo and behold no lump was found. A mammogram confirmed to my very perplexed gynecologist that the lump he had felt just three weeks before was nowhere to be found.

Was the lump a figment of both my and my gynecologist's imagination? Or was my faith in the Lord and his Mother Mary, as well as the use of the oil and prayer my salvation? I may never know for sure, but I like to think it was all of the above. Nowadays I pray the rosary every chance I get—sometimes several times a day. I truly believe God touched me and woke up my heart and my faith. He changed my life for the better. For now I know that if you truly believe, God and His angels will be there.

An Angel Named Ray

McKenzie
New Jersey

As I lay in my bed looking around my hospital room, I wondered: *How did I ever end up here?* Never in a million years did I ever think that I would be fighting for my life at the young age of thirty-two. Looking back now, I can only tell you that there is one answer to how I got there: GOD!

You truly have to hear my story and understand my situation in order to fully appreciate and believe that it was all in God's plan. I've always believed that God has a plan for everything, and now I know firsthand that He does. God truly works in mysterious ways.

I am the mother of two young boys who are the love of my life. After the birth of my youngest, I never stopped bleeding vaginally. During my delivery there was quite a struggle to remove my placenta. After six weeks I went for my routine checkup and was prescribed a medication for two days. This medication was supposed to contract

my uterus and help to push out any remaining placenta that could be causing the bleeding. After two days, however, there was no change so I was put on the medication again for another two. Still there was no change. Two more weeks had passed now making it a total of eight weeks since I had given birth, and the bleeding continued.

Then one afternoon, I felt a "pop" on my right temple and instantly had the most excruciating headache. I took two Advil hoping to allevi-

McKenzie (left), Ray Skop, and Mary.

ate the pain, but it didn't work. That same night we had plans to have dinner with my in-laws who live about an hour away from us. We went ahead with our plans, thinking that the pain would just diminish over time, even though my head continued to throb. Before we left my in-laws to make the trip home, I took more Advil, but again it didn't help. When we arrived back home that night, I put the kids to sleep and went to bed early hoping that some rest would help. But when I woke up a few hours later to nurse my baby, I was faced with another problem—I was hemorrhaging. Something was terribly wrong.

I then called my ob-gyn who told me to go straight to the ER. She explained that they would probably have to do a D&C which is a procedure in which they scrape the uterus to remove anything that shouldn't be there. When I arrived, I was immediately given a bed. The nurse then drew some blood. The result was astonishing. The test revealed that I was pregnant!

To say that I was shocked is an understatement. How could this be?

My son was just eight weeks old! My HCG level, which is a pregnancy hormone, was sky high. In fact, it was at 230,000. A normal pregnant woman has levels between 60,000 and 100,000. I honestly didn't know what to think. I wasn't pregnant, yet my body still thought it was. As I sat there trying to digest all of this data, the pain in my head began to intensify. The doctor, observing my increasing discomfort, ordered an ultrasound and CT scan to be performed immediately.

After the scan, I was asked if I had had any trauma to my head over the last two weeks. I replied, "No." At this point my head was spinning, and the words that I heard from the doctors were bleeding on the brain and a possible brain aneurysm. These words were frightening. The doctors needed further assurance that their diagnosis was accurate and what they had to do to save my life. An MRI was scheduled and performed. The MRI determined that there was a tumor on my brain with a pocket of blood surrounding it. In fact, the MRI discovered multiple tumors on my brain and a few in my lungs. The result was emergency brain surgery without hesitation.

I was in a swirling vortex of bad news. Why is this happening to me? Oh God, why me? All of the "what ifs" captured my thoughts. What if I didn't survive the surgery? What if I was handicapped as a result of this surgery? Who would take care of my family? I prayed as I have never prayed before. I put my affairs in order with the Lord and put all my physical and mental efforts on survival. I was going to survive. I was going to be the person I was yesterday. I was not going to be handicapped. I was going to beat this. I cannot say I was not scared beyond belief. Facing death is never a pleasant place to be, but I was not going to die. I was going to survive and I was going to be a strong survivor. I was going to play with my boys after this. I planned our activities to include riding bikes, playing ball, swimming, biking, and a lot of quality time together. I was going to watch them grow up. I was going to grow old with my husband. The surgery was performed—successfully, thank the Lord.

The next few days were spent in the Intensive Care Unit recovering and being monitored for complications. I heard a knock at the door. I had a visitor. A man entered my room and stepped close to my bed. He introduced himself as the hospital chaplain. He explained that he is not only a pastor but also a cancer survivor who shares his enlightening story with others. He is very inspiring and his mission is to help others cope with their physical challenges and know that there is always hope. He is an angel who came into my life, giving me strength, motivation and a path to survival.

My healing continued while my doctors planned the treatment to eliminate the disease that inhabited my body. Once they had their plan, they then explained to me that within the next few weeks I was going to need an extensive regimen of radiation and chemotherapy, not knowing when or how this would end. After all, I was battling Stage 4 cancer with a very strong positive attitude.

Then one day after I was cleared to go to a regular room on the oncology floor, I had an unexpected visitor named Mary. She was the start of my spiritual journey. As she entered my overly crowded room, she met my family and made her way to my bedside. She said only that she didn't know me but was asked to visit me by a special person in my life. She then asked if I minded if she prayed over me. I certainly had no issue with this; I welcomed her prayers. As she prayed aloud, the whole room joined in prayer. My incision began to tingle instantly where Mary had applied oil which I came to learn was the blessed oil that weeps from Ray Skop's picture of Mother Mary. I now realized that I was in the midst of a life-changing spiritual experience. I felt absolute love in my room, and it was a feeling such as I have never felt before. When Mary finished praying with us, she explained that she had a friend with whom she wanted me to speak. She said that his name was Ray and he lived in Jersey City.

Mary continued to describe this incredible man and share stories of his many miraculous healings. To hear such amazing stories was very reassuring, but how was I going to get to Jersey City? Mary asked me if I felt strong enough to speak with Ray right now because he was awaiting my call. This was my introduction to the complete restoration of not only my faith but the faith of my family. Mary called Ray and allowed the whole room to hear the conversation. The words coming from this stranger were so comforting. He had never met me, but he spoke to me as though we had known each other for years. There are many things I cannot recall from that conversation, but the words I heard Ray speak that carried me through my illness were "McKenzie, you're going to be fine." My family, who had remained in my room throughout this experience, indeed felt something had just happened which was very moving. We now know how on point Ray's words were. We closed our conversation with Ray who offered a prayer for me and asked me to call him the next day.

From that day forward, my conversations with Ray were daily. The subject matter was never the same. We discussed anything and everything. Our conversations were not always about faith and healing. Often he would speak with my husband about their mutual interests, or his grandchildren would get on the phone to say hello and sometimes even sing me a song. What I learned from all of these conversations is that Ray is a genuine, caring, and sharing regular guy. He has had a variety of experiences. While chatting about some of his experiences, he told me how people often know only one side of him. "I was in the diner and one person called me holy man while another called me Harley man," he once told me. Yes, Ray is so regular he enjoys riding his Harley with his son Ray and friends while making time to help those in need. Our conversations always ended with Ray saying a prayer for me and my family. Each prayer was unique and totally spontaneous. Each prayer was on point for that day and was special to me.

It wasn't until months later that my health permitted me to meet Ray face to face at his Rosary House. The Rosary House is as the name suggests just that—a home dedicated to Mother Mary, honoring her by bringing people together devoted to saying the rosary. They come to pray, visit, and get to know one another. The Rosary House has a fraternal feel where initiation is by adoration of Mother Mary and devotion to the rosary. The group is tight knit but not a private closed group. Their prayers are freely given and affect a multitude of those in need. Ray has introduced me to many of the rosary house regulars over the phone. They have sung songs to me, shared personal experiences, and prayed with me and for me. I was also introduced to other cancer survivors who have received Ray's help. My chance meeting with Ray through Mary was and is a life-changing, enlightening, and spiritual involvement. I know in my heart that Ray is more than just a normal man in Jersey City helping people. He is a special human being doing the work of the Lord in humble and nondescript surroundings while serving people in need.

From the first time that I spoke with Ray, he reassured me that I was going to be okay. I never doubted him. Ray not only inspired me but also taught me to trust and believe truly in the power of prayer. Today I am in complete remission. If I lived forever, I would never be able to thank enough all of the people who had helped me. I've learned through this blip in my life that angels do take many forms. Luckily, I have had the good fortune of having many angels visit me in my life. Ray is one of those angels. I have also learned that the combination of the best treatment and powerful prayers cannot be beat. I am both inspired and motivated to move on with my life and help others just as others have come forward and helped me during my time of greatest need. Ray is my "Ray of Hope" and the "Ray of Hope" for many, many others.

An Afterthought

As noted earlier, I don't believe my meeting Ray was an accident. I will never forget how nervous I was when Ray began telling me about how he can often "see through" people, and he immediately knows whether or not they have good intentions at heart. "Josie," he said, "So many people come in here claiming that they are good people or that they want to help others, but I can see through this. I can tell whether or not you are a good person."

Honestly, I could feel my heart beating heavily against my chest as I thought, "OH MY GOD, he can see my sins. He knows I'm not perfect." Then suddenly, as though he was reading my mind, Ray put a reassuring hand on my shoulder and smiled saying, "Josie, you have a good heart. I know you are doing this for the right reason." I can't begin to tell you how much those words meant to me. In fact, it was then that I knew Ray was meant to be in this book and that our meeting was not by chance.

Ray never takes credit for the many miracles which have been attributed to him, saying always that it is up to God, not him. The day I met Ray I was immediately awestruck by his humble demeanor, noting that he was just a regular guy who enjoys fishing and just spending time with his family. At one point I asked him if he was always religious. To this he just chuckled, saying "Oh, no!" Before 1998 Ray admittedly was more interested in riding his Harley Davidson than going to church or saying the rosary. And when I asked Ray why God chose him to do the work that he now does, I couldn't help but laugh myself when he replied, "I have no idea."

Having met Ray, though, I think he was chosen because he is someone whom we can all relate to. No, he is not perfect by any means, but he does have love in his heart and a strong desire to do God's work and to help others. Many people have asked me whether or not I believe if angels walk among us. In response, I can truthfully say that I certainly do believe angels walk among us. Angels come in many forms, and to me Ray is one of them.

Addendum

An Angel Goes Home

Don't be dismayed by goodbyes. A farewell is necessary before you can meet again. And meeting again, after moments or lifetimes, is certain for those who are friends.   Richard Bach

One of the most difficult questions in life is why bad things happen to good people. Let's face it—the world is full of pain and suffering. And when things go wrong, the first question many ask is why, God? Why? I found myself asking this very same question over and over again when my wonderful friend Ray suffered a stroke.

A faith healer, Ray dedicated his life to unselfishly helping others. His phone was always ringing with people who needed his help, and he never refused anyone. I am proud to have had the privilege of knowing him and calling him my friend.

He suffered a stroke Monday, June 18, 2012, and though I was both stunned and saddened by the news, I held on to hope that he would recover. The following day at about 2:45 a.m., I went to bed and said a prayer for Ray. Afterwards, immediately upon closing my eyes, I saw a vision of him. He looked so happy and was waving hello to me repeatedly saying "Hi, Josie! Hi, Josie!" He was smiling and appeared much younger and thinner, wearing what seemed to be a denim jacket. He also looked as if he was surrounded by beautiful trees and grass.

To be honest, I was afraid of what I saw for two reasons. For one, I was completely awake and second, I knew if this really was my friend, he had crossed over. I opened my eyes quickly and then noticed that there was a chill near the right side of my

The author with Ray Skop

face. I touched the left side of my face and it felt warm, yet I could feel a chill on the right side.

When the spirit of loved ones is around, we will often feel a cold sensation. Spirits often use up some of the energy in the room which causes cold spots. Knowing this, I intuitively knew that my friend was present that night.

Thinking of Ray, I closed my eyes for a second time and again saw him smiling at me. I quickly opened my eyes again wondering if he was stopping by to say goodbye to me. I then closed my eyes for a third time, but this time I did not see Ray and the chill was no longer there. I had a hard time sleeping that night because I was worried about my friend but eventually fell asleep. The next morning I feared that I was going to get a phone call telling me that Ray had passed.

Although, thankfully, I did not get that phone call, I was told that he was in critical condition. This was all so heartbreaking. Ray was at the helm of many incredible miracles and divine interventions. As I said, he had dedicated his life to helping others.

Ray never regained consciousness and passed on July 3, 2012. Although I am deeply saddened because I will miss his physical presence, I am happy for him because I know he is now happy. I guess you can say I am happy for him but sad for me. I had only just met Ray in December 2011, yet we shared a connection I cannot explain. I'll never forget one of the conversations I had with Ray when he said, "Josie, I want us to be good friends." I smiled back at him feeling honored by his words and said, "Me, too, Ray." I just never thought our friendship would be so short lived. In my mind we had forever, but forever was not to be.

Yes, our friendship will continue as I know Ray will always be there for me in spirit. But, still, I find myself wishing we had had more time. I wish I had made more of an effort to go to Jersey City to spend time with him. I wish I had called him more often. The list goes on. Sadly, most of us don't think of these things until our loved ones are no longer with us. It's a hard way to learn that we should never take anything in life for granted. If you love someone, say it. If you care, show it. Let your friends know how much they are appreciated. You may never get the chance tomorrow for all you are guaranteed is right now.

So why do bad things happen to good people? Why did God take such a beautiful man who was needed so much and who made such a difference in the lives of countless others, including my own? I don't know why. But what I do know is there is a reason for everything. Nothing happens without purpose.

I also know that God, Supreme Being, or whatever you choose to call him is all loving and infinite. The book of Job tells the story of how Job, a very wealthy man, lost everything. Although Job is under-standably upset and questions why such bad things happened to him, he never loses his faith. Job knows that God is good and therefore continues to trust in him. This story is a lesson for us all. When bad things happen, we need to hold on to that faith and trust.

Truthfully, I don't understand why Ray had to leave us. But I also know that some things are not meant for us to understand.

I once read a story about a twenty-five-year-old son with cerebral palsy who prayed to God asking that his deceased mom come to him. Suddenly he saw a vision of his mother. As the story goes, she told her son that she had to leave him so that he would learn to do things on his own. This story was a reminder to me that we are all here to learn lessons. Once those lessons are learned and our purpose for being here is met, we go home.

Heaven welcomed home an angel. Our loved ones can and do continue to watch over us and help us from the Other Side. Although I am deeply saddened, it brings me comfort to know that Ray has now gotten his wings and will continue to help others. Although we needed him here, heaven needed him more.

This book is dedicated in loving memory of my friend Ray. For information, please visit <u>www.rayofhopefoundation.com</u>.

We Are Never Alone

Thus far you've read several stories about angelic and divine encounters. But were they angels who intervened or spirit guides? Is there a difference?

Some believe that angels are not in the same category as spirit guides. Angels, they say, do not take human form while spirit guides, however, once lived on this earth. They may be deceased relatives or friends who have agreed to watch over us.

As I explained earlier in my introduction, I believe that angels and spirit guides are the same thing. There are definitely different levels of spirit guides and angels, but they are the same thing because their purpose is one and the same. Think of it this way: There is a riot in your hometown and several police officers arrive on the scene to help. Do you point out that this policeman is a lieutenant while that one over there is only a rookie? No, they are all police officers with the same purpose: to help and to serve.

Renowned psychic medium, James Van Praagh, agrees that angels and guides are one and the same. In his book *Talking to Heaven*, he

explains how we will draw three different types of guides to us depending on our needs. They are, according to Van Praagh, personal
guides, specialized helpers, and master teachers. The first group, he
notes, are people we have known in previous incarnations with whom
we share a kinship or similarity. These personal guides often help us
by putting thoughts in our minds.

When I set out to write *Visits from Heaven* which contains evidential
afterlife-communication accounts from around the world, I had one
message in mind: Life never ends and love never dies. The bonds of
love can never be broken. People always ask me if their loved ones
know what is going on in their lives. Yes, they are very much aware of
what is going on.

In fact, a loved one on the Other Side may even decide to be your
personal guide. A personal guide can be someone you knew in your
current lifetime. It could be, for example, a parent, grandparent, sib-
ling, friend, cousin, aunt, or uncle.

My friend Cyndi was in a horrific car accident. Although she suf-
fered serious injuries, she did survive. Sadly, her friend Linda was
killed. Years later, Cyndi was offered a reading with a psychic medium.
The reading went very well, and Cyndi received several validations.
However, there is one thing that was said in this reading that struck
Cyndi most of all.

This psychic medium surprised Cyndi by telling her that she had a
guardian angel with her at all times. She went on to describe this
guardian angel's physical appearance and even gave Cyndi a name.
The angel was none other than Linda, the friend who had died in that
fateful car accident years earlier. So, again, our loved ones are very
much aware of what is going on in our lives. Many even guide and
help us with everyday decision making and events.

James Van Praagh explains, "Personal guides may make vigorous
attempts to guide us through our daily lives and impress us with the
best way to remedy certain situations. However, at the same time it is
important to note that these loved ones cannot and do not interfere
with those lessons or challenges that we have created on earth from
which to learn and grow. Our learning process is never an easy one,
and in order for us to get the most benefit from a particular situation
or life lesson, many times these guides just stand by and watch us

make decisions. Even though at times it seems things are unbearable, it is at those times that we learn the most.

"Many people ask if our guides are with us all the time or whether we have to reach out to them and ask them to come through. My answer is: We are never alone. Our guides are with us always. Their spiritual task is to watch over us and assist us. Our guides may change from time to time depending on the task in which we are involved. But we never need to call them, for they know our needs and are always ready to lend us a hand." (pgs. 43–4)

As an example, you have an important meeting the next day and set your alarm clock. When morning comes, you wake up frustrated because you realize that your alarm clock did not go off. You hurry out of bed and rush to get dressed but fall on your way to the bathroom. Finally, you get to your car and drive off, only to hit traffic at every turn. Every driver in front of you appears to be on the slow boat to China. As you near the office complex, you are confronted with emergency personnel. A tractor trailer overturned, causing a ten-car pileup, and several people were injured. Could you have been one of them had you not had all these annoying interruptions?

I know this example seems a bit extreme, but this is how guidance from spirit works. Their guidance is very delicate and indirect. They don't scream at us and tell us what to do. If they did, we'd probably all run for cover. Rather, they give us subtle messages or hints. It's up to us to get the message. Recently, my family and I went to see a house in town which was for sale. I had a bit of a stomach ache before I left my house but brushed it off. When we arrived, we all loved the street and were very impressed with the homes in the area. Once inside the house, my husband went on and on about how impressed he was and how he felt we should buy the house.

There was something about this house that didn't sit well with me, but I just figured it was due to my being overly cautious and picky. We walked into the kitchen and unbeknownst to me, there was a step leading to the family room. I didn't see the step and tripped and fell. I brushed it off and just continued on with the tour of the house.

Moments later, my husband and our realtor called me over to take a look at the huge attic. I walked up the steps, got to the top, and fell hard. At this point, I was hurting and very frustrated. I pulled my husband John aside and said, "I fell twice in this house. They (my angels and spirits guides) are telling me something. This is not the house for us." My husband really wanted to buy this home, and I know he is still disappointed with me. But I also know spirit was telling me that it was not meant to be. Why? I don't know. Maybe in the long run we would not have been able to afford the house. Again, I don't know for sure. But looking back, my gut tells me that we made the right decision by not buying that house.

And speaking of gut, spirit guides often communicate with us by those gut or nagging feelings that we get. Years ago, my husband John was offered two jobs. One was a great job opportunity with Cantor Fitzgerald, a well-known investment firm then at the World Trade Center in New York City. The position was a high-level management job and would have given him a substantial pay increase. Plus, he would be working for his former boss and friend, someone he highly admired and respected.

After thinking about it, John (to my surprise) decided not to take the offer. When I asked him why, he told me that something was telling him not to take the Cantor Fitzgerald position. To be honest I was so disappointed and shocked because I felt it was a terrific opportunity for him and we could certainly use the money. I even told him that he was crazy and should take the position with Cantor Fitzgerald. But John felt strongly about his decision and went with the other investment firm.

Many months later, Cantor Fitzgerald and all of its employees in that office perished in the World Trade Center attacks on September 11, 2001. This is a day that will live on in history—never to be forgotten. Had my husband listened to me and not his gut, I would have been widowed.

The next type of guides, says Van Praagh, are called mastery or specialized helpers. These spirit guides are drawn to us based on the work we are involved in. As a writer, I often ask for assistance with my work. I can't begin to tell you how many times I have been stuck with writer's block and then an idea will come to me seemingly out of nowhere. It is said that our thoughts draw to us those guides who have the specific expertise to assist us.

Why do angels and spirit guides help us? There is an easy answer.

"It is the way," explains Van Praagh. "When we pass into the world of spirit we become keenly aware that we are all equally one. We want to help humankind to grow, to learn, to share ideas, to better itself. By impressing their thoughts upon humans and aiding them, spiritual guides help humankind to tune into the spiritual force in all things. Again, depending on how open we are, spirit inspirations may be exceptional and awe-inspiring, or they might be patiently waiting for the day when they are noticed." (pgs. 44–5)

The third level of spirit guides or helpers, notes Van Praagh, is known as spirit or master teachers. These master teachers may be highly spiritually evolved. Some may have been involved in spiritual work while they lived on this earth during many lifetimes. Others may never have incarnated. These spirit guides are there to help us with our spiritual progression or path to enlightenment.

"Most of us will have one or two of the same master teachers throughout our soul's evolution lifetime after lifetime," Van Praagh writes in conclusion. "These beings are tuned into our spiritual selves and will help us to grow spiritually throughout our time on the physical plane, as well as assist us in between lives. In addition, we will have individual master guides during a particular lifetime. Once again, based on our soul's evolution, a guide is drawn to us to help with important lessons or aspects of our personalities that need to be perfected. For example, we might have a guide to assist us in learning unconditional love. Or a master guide may help us in lessons about selfishness. The saying 'When the student is ready, the teacher will appear' is quite true." (pg. 45)

One of my readers once sent me a private message on Facebook. "Josie, they say we all have angels and spirit guides. Is this true? If so, why is everything going wrong in my life?" I wrote this woman back and asked her if she sought help from her angels and spirit guides. I wanted to know if she prayed and asked for their help. Her response was, "No."

I wrote back to her explaining how many times when things are seemingly going wrong in our lives it's an indication that we are off course. We are not following the path in this lifetime which will teach us the lessons we came here to learn. I encouraged her to pray for guidance. I'm not saying that those who don't pray or seek help won't receive divine guidance. Most of the time the subtle messages or guidance that we receive go unnoticed, but that doesn't mean that our spiritual helpers are not there. They are always there for us.

Truthfully, we are never alone. Someone is always there, watching over us, but they will not interfere with the lessons we need to learn. Everything happens for a reason and nothing is without purpose.

Although our guides send us signs or help us, we still have free will. We can either stop and listen to that intuitive voice within and follow the guidance that we receive or we can ignore it. They are always there to lend us a hand; we need only be open to receiving their help. We need only take the time to stop and listen. It's our choice.

*Excerpts were taken from James Van Praagh's book *Talking to Heaven: A Medium's Message of Life after Death.* New York: Dutton (Published by the Penguin Group), 1997.

A Grandmother's Love

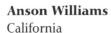

Anson Williams
California

Love is the one thing that tran-
scends death. In fact, it's the very
reason we are all here—to love
and be loved. It is the very essence of our being. And when we
finally cross over and make our
transition to the Other Side, we
will take the bonds of love that
we shared with people on this earth with us.

People often ask me if their loved one is upset with them on the
Other Side because of something that happened before they died. My
answer is always, "No!" When we cross over, there is no hatred, judgment, jealousy, or anger. There is only understanding, compassion, and
love.

While it's true that our deceased loved ones have moved on to another dimension, it doesn't mean that they are no longer with us. We are all spiritual beings having a human experience, and when we die, we shed our bodies and go back to being spirit. We are all made up of energy and this energy never dies, it only shifts form.

We are all connected by this very energy and love. Since this love surpasses death, it makes sense that our loved ones would want to continue to help us and guide us. The connection that we share continues to draw our loved ones to us whenever we need them, much the same way it does those still here on earth. Not surprisingly, then, those on the Other Side may choose to act as a spirit guide for someone they love here on earth. Often times this involves saving us from a dangerous situation.

Actor, director, and producer Anson Williams became a household name when he landed the role of "Potsie" in the hit television series *Happy Days*. The iconic show premiered in January 1974 and ran for eleven seasons. Williams eventually stepped behind the camera producing and/or directing several films and television shows such as *Melrose Place, Star Trek: Voyager, Xena: Warrior Princess, Hercules: The Legendary Journeys, Sabrina the Teenage Witch,* and *Charmed.* He also appeared in *Happy Days* reunion specials. An entrepreneur and businessman, he founded a cosmetics company called Starmaker Products (www.starmakerproducts.com) and is also a featured speaker.

Despite his success, one of his life's most memorable moments has nothing to do with his fame or impressive show business career but has everything to do with the love of his grandmother, a woman who passed away before he was born. The following is Williams' story in his own words:

> The paranormal was discussed a lot in my family. My mother had natural psychic ability. She never charged for it and she never exploited it, but word of mouth spread it around. It had brought quite a few people to the house. I was around it most of my life.
>
> My parents were very normal people. They were not strange or off. This was just part of their life. My father was a tech illustrator, and my mother was a homemaker. My mom and dad told me that when I was a baby, they would go into my room and see an image

of my grandmother, almost as if she was protecting me by my bed. Before I was born, she died in her mid-40s from breast cancer. They would see what looked like a soft photograph floating by my bed. It wasn't like a ghost, but more like an angel. It was calming and peaceful by my bed, almost like an inner light. Even though I never met her, I had a good feeling of what she was about.

I believe it was 1971; I finally could afford my first new car. It was a yellow VW which back then wasn't exactly the safest car, but it was the cheapest. I was driving on Burbank Boulevard in Burbank, California and going over an overpass.

I had picked up a stray German shepherd on the street. It had no tags and no collar so I decided to take the dog to the pound. Instead of sitting on the seat on the passenger side, the dog ended up sitting underneath the seat where leg room is. I came to this intersection and was waiting to make a left hand turn. Cars were going by.

Suddenly, in the corner of my eye, I saw a car run the red light. The woman seemed to be looking behind her at her kids or something. At about 35-40 miles per hour, she hit me full force on the passenger side. The same side the dog was on. The collision was enough to nearly rip the car in half. I didn't have a seatbelt on. At the moment of impact, my head hit the rearview mirror, and I was headed toward the front window. At this moment I saw the face of my Grandmother Ann. She was smiling at me, and it was very angelic and beautiful. She had beautiful blue eyes and very light skin. She gave me the most comforting look and the kindest smile.

The experience was very comforting and as real as it could be. In fact, I remember everything that happened all the way through. It was almost like stop-action photography. My grandmother looked at me and said, "Everything is fine." And I immediately knew that everything was going to be fine. I remember everything about it. It almost felt as if something was pushing me back. It also felt as if an hour had passed. But then time happened again.

My car was annihilated—almost like a can; it was just pulled apart. On the passenger's side, the car was peeled up. When the police came, they thought for sure that someone had died. But I was fine and the dog was fine. If the dog had been on the seat, it would have been killed. But because he was on the floor, it was almost like a bubble formed to protect the dog.

The paramedics thought I had to be really hurt. They kept checking me and asking me how I was. But I kept saying that I was not hurt and that I was fine. All I had was a scratch on my head. I was taken by ambulance to the hospital and they did a series of tests and nothing—I was fine.

My grandmother had felt so real that I knew that I was okay. I felt it. I felt protected. When I told my mother and father, they felt it was very valid. They understood. They believed what I believed.

My father and I had to go down to the yard where they towed the car and my dad started crying when he saw the car. He couldn't believe how damaged the car was and that I had lived through it. I know my grandmother saved my life. There's definitely something beyond now. What it is? How it is? I'll embrace that when the time comes. But for now I know there's something more.

A Helping Hand from Heaven

Most of us don't even think twice about praying to God or another Supreme Being to help those on the Other Side. But what many don't realize is that we can also pray directly to our deceased loved ones. They are actually of more help to us in spirit than they ever were in body. And sometimes they even solicit the help of someone here on earth to give them a helping hand.

In September 2011 I started a page on Facebook based on my book *Visits from Heaven*. My reasoning was to give people a place where they could come to share their own spiritually transformative experiences (STEs) without fear of being judged. I wanted the bereaved to understand that life never ends and love never dies. Members of my page know that they are not alone because they are able to read the experiences of so many others.

The page quickly took off and people started to post accounts. It had been up only about two weeks when a bereaved mother named Lisa posted on September 24, 2011, an incredible story about her deceased son Richie. Below is the account in her own words:

257

My youngest son committed suicide on March 7 of this year. I was so grief-stricken that I could barely function. I decided that maybe a medium might help and spent two months searching for the right person on the Internet. When I finally narrowed my search, I just could not bring myself to make the call. Then, on the night of May 19, I had the most incredible dream. Honestly, I have never experienced anything like this before. I dreamed that my son was giving me a tour through heaven. There were symbols and the most unbelievable auras around the doorways. Everything was three dimensional. The colors were so vivid and unbelievably beautiful.

I have a very hard time sleeping, and since I never sleep well, I almost never have dreams. Or if I do, I never remember them. With this dream, however, I woke up recalling every detail, especially the beautiful auras that encircled some sort of Asian or Indian symbols. I honestly had this sense that my son had just given me a tour of heaven and was telling me he was happy and in a good place. This dream inspired me to pick up the phone, and I made a call to Glenn Klausner (a psychic medium). I left a message, and to my amazement he called back and I actually had my reading that day. Four of my family members came through, and he explained that my son was in transition.

Glenn then started to talk about my other son Jason and shared that he was going to have a "Christopher Reeves" type of an accident to his neck and for me not to worry; he would be just fine. He asked me if the 19th or 24th meant anything—they did not at the time. Then Glenn started to talk to me about something called a chakra (I had no idea what this was so I wrote down the word and decided to look it up later). After the reading, I started to cry because I was so disappointed that Richie did not come through. As the days passed, I finally did an Internet search on the word chakra. I clicked and stared down at the screen and was spellbound seeing the same symbols and the same vivid colors that were in my epic dream. I then looked down at my notes from the reading and noticed that the 19th had been the night of this epic dream.

Then this past July we decided to take our son's car but noticed it was low on gas. Before we left for the gas station, my husband checked the key for the gas cap and it worked perfectly. However, when we arrived at the gas station, the cap would just not open so we searched for a second key in the glove compartment. At the bottom of the glove compartment was a penny with a document sticking up so I pulled it out and looked at it. It was the bulletin from a church our son had visited when he had accepted Jesus Christ into his life on May 24, 2010. A few moments after I read this note, the gas cap door suddenly sprang open. Then on August 4, we received a call from my daughter telling us that our oldest son Jason had been taken to the emergency room. He was working towards his black belt in Jujutsu. As he was doing choke holds, he tore the main artery in the back of his neck and suffered a stroke.

I prayed to God, "Please do not take both of my boys. Losing another son would be just too much to bear." It had not dawned on me until my daughter mentioned it that this was the prediction that Glenn had told me about on May 20. I had this sense of calm as Glenn also said my son would be okay. At the time of my son's stroke, he could not talk or even swallow water. His eyes were rolling back, and he wasn't able to even focus. He could not walk. Despite the odds, he was back to normal in less than four weeks. I believe that although Richie did not come through during my reading, he sent the message that he would be our guardian angel and that he was watching over his brother. I believe Richie kept his brother safe.

Lisa
Washington

As I read Lisa's post on my *Visits from Heaven* Facebook page, I kept thinking about the penny she mentioned in her story. Something or someone was telling me to tell Lisa to pay attention to the date of the penny she had found in the glove compartment of her deceased son's car. I had no idea if Lisa still had the penny or if she would even listen to me, but for some reason, I had to try to get a hold of her.

I decided, therefore, to post a comment on my page asking Lisa to please email me. She did contact me on Sunday, September 25, but I was on the road and emailed Lisa back via my BlackBerry to tell her that I would send a reply to her email later that evening. My hope was to share a story explaining how pennies can be used as a sign from heaven so that she would then pay attention to the date on the penny she had found that day. But, again, I had no idea if she even still had this penny.

That evening I was watching television with my husband and two daughters. Suddenly, the electricity went out briefly for about five seconds. My husband and I didn't think anything of it and passed it off as a fluke thing since the electricity quickly came back on. About an hour later after putting my two daughters to bed, I told my husband John that I had to go to my home office and send out an email. I proceeded to write Lisa, explaining how pennies can be significant signs from heaven and asking her if she had taken notice of the date on the penny found in her son's glove compartment.

As I neared the end of my email, the power suddenly went out again causing me to lose what I had just spent a long time typing. Frustrated but feeling as though I needed to get this note to Lisa, I rebooted my computer and started typing up another email. Again, to my dismay, just as I neared completion of my letter, the power went out for a third time. Naturally, I was upset and I told my husband that someone did not want me to send this email out. I then said out loud, "Okay, fine. I get it. I guess you don't want me to send this out tonight!" Irritated, I then went to bed.

I woke up the next morning thinking about Lisa. For reasons I cannot explain, I couldn't get her out of my mind and had a great urge to email her. Typically, my workday doesn't start until I come home from taking my kids to school. But on this day, I got up early and once again tried to send Lisa an email urging her to pay attention to the date on that penny. Thankfully, there were no more power outages, and I was able to send my email without incident.

A short time later, I received a reply from Lisa. She thanked me for my note and said she did indeed still have that penny but never paid any attention to the date. She would check the date and get back to me. Shortly after, I received this reply from Lisa:

OH MY LORD, I am in shock! You are not going to believe the date that is on that penny! It is 1975 which was the year my oldest son (Jason) was born.[9] He is my son who had the stroke!

When I received her email, I read and reread her note feeling stunned that my intuition was correct in telling her to pay attention to that penny, but I also couldn't shake off the feeling that there was more to it. The next day I received yet another email from Lisa—an email that would bring me to tears and prove that our loved ones are looking after us and sometimes solicit the help of others on earth. Here's what Lisa wrote:

I am convinced that something powerful was keeping you from sending that email to me Sunday night as it would not have had an impact on Sunday as it did on Monday. Let me share with you what happened yesterday. On Sunday night something very weird happened. I am actually not sure what this was as it seemed like I was in a conscious state the entire night . . . I honestly do not think I was in a dreamlike state. Anyway, someone kept waking me up, telling me something had happened to my oldest son Jason. When I turned to look at the clock, it said 1:21 a.m. (This is my son Jason's birthdate). I rolled over and the same thing happened, but this time it was my daughter shaking me to awake up, saying something had happened to Jason.

Then all of a sudden my husband woke me out of a sound sleep about 7 a.m. yesterday morning, saying something about a message from Jay. He kept saying something about Jay. I was thinking, *Oh my God, what happened to Jason?* He was actually talking about our attorney in St. Croix, but it really scared the daylights out of me.

I had overslept and we were late for an appointment, but I was drawn to go to my computer and that was when I found your email telling me to check the date of the penny. My husband was furious

---

[9]**Author's Note:** When our loved ones on the Other Side leave us pennies or other coins as a sign from heaven, they are typically either the year of their birth or the year of their passing.

with me because we were so late for this appointment. I just ignored what he said and told him I had to check the date of the penny first. When I was writing to you, I had this nagging feeling that something was wrong or about to happen to my son again. So on the way to our appointment, I called him and had this anxious feeling something was wrong when he did not answer the phone as he normally picks up on the first ring. I then began to panic. I called my daughter and then Jason's wife Stephanie, telling her that I was very worried about Jason and that I just could not explain why. Stephanie is a school teacher so she could not call back but sent me a text message that they had had an argument about him going back to Jujutsu and that Jason would go behind her back and do it anyway even when the doctor had told him not to because it was too dangerous.

About ten minutes later, I received a call from my son telling me he was just fine. I asked where he was and he said he was working on a job and shared that he had been on a sixteen-foot ladder and on a roof, adding a new electric panel for a client. I told him to be very careful today that I was getting a sense he might be in some sort of danger. I sent him your email and told him to please read the story you shared with me about pennies and sent him a copy of a photo I had taken of the 1975 penny along with background of finding the penny in Richie's car.

Then about 9 p.m. last night my son called to share what had transpired after we spoke. He was extra cautious about getting back on the sixteen-foot ladder and said to himself that this ladder really needs to be replaced. He was working at a restaurant and had to walk across a very old tin roof to get to the electrical panel. Just as he was about to take a step towards the panel, he noticed a shiny penny on the roof where he was working and picked it up. This is what is amazing! He said that if he had not stopped to pick up the penny and had taken the next step forward, he would have fallen through the roof. Jason later explained to me that in his mind, he knew the roof was not safe but figured he had no choice because he had to run new wire across it. When he leaned down to pick up the penny, he noticed that the rafters just ahead of him were broken and split. If he had taken another step, the roof would not have supported his weight and he would have fallen through. Jason had not read your story until he got home from work and said that after reading your story and seeing his birthdate on the penny, he felt he was receiving a message not to take any more risks with his life. He promised me that he would not be going back to the Jujutsu studio and would find another sport.

Thank you again for sharing the story about the penny. You may actually have saved my son's life yesterday.

Lisa
Washington

As I read Lisa's words, I couldn't control myself as the tears began to flow endlessly. "You may actually have saved my son's life yesterday." I stared at her words in utter amazement as I thought about how everything had unfolded. Richie had used me to get a message to his mother and as a result protected his brother Jason. I was in total shock and wanted to talk to Lisa by phone.

Later that night, I called Lisa, and we talked about what had happened. As we spoke, Lisa mentioned something about an electrical panel on the roof. "What a minute, Lisa!" I said interrupting her.

"You said your son was on the roof working, right?"

"Yes," she replied.

"Lisa, what does your son do for a living?"

"He's an electrician," she answered.

At this point, my heart was racing. I literally felt like I wanted to jump out of my skin. "LISA!" I shouted into the phone. Your son is an ELECTRICIAN. MY ELECTRICITY WENT OUT THREE TIMES the night I tried to send you my email!

We were both flabbergasted and stunned as we realized that Richie was the one keeping me from sending out that email until the next morning. It was one of the most incredible validations I have ever experienced proving that our loved ones are still there for us. Yet again, this story shows that nothing can ever break the bonds of love—not even death.

𝓕inal Thoughts

Many divine interventions and miracles have been said to have taken place in Lourdes, France ever since the Virgin Mary reportedly appeared there in February 1858 to a young girl named Bernadette. Perhaps one of the most remarkable stories is that of Dr. Alexis Carrel.

Carrel, a Nobel Prize winning surgeon, biologist, and renowned skeptic, was on a train ride to Lourdes when he was asked to care for a woman named Marie-Louise Bally who was in the final stage of terminal tuberculosis. Despite the severity of her illness, she reportedly insisted on making the trip. Once they arrived, Carrel watched as water from the shrine was poured over her large tumor-filled abdomen. He continued to watch in astonishment as this deathly ill woman began to improve before his very eyes, and her once swollen stomach flattened out.

A transformed believer, he later wrote about his experience in a book titled *Journey to Lourdes*.

At first Carrel struggled with the miracle he had witnessed because it was not explainable by scientific law. Like eighteenth century Scottish philosopher David Hume, he had believed that no evidence would be sufficient to effectively and scientifically demonstrate a miracle. But Carrel, of course, was proven wrong when he, himself, witnessed a miraculous cure that had no other logical explanation.

Dutch-born philosopher Baruch Spinoza takes quite a different stance on the issue of miracles. According to Spinoza, it is not that miracles take place outside the laws of nature but only outside of laws we currently understand. In other words, how do we know that these miracles are not actually within the laws of nature, just not the way we understand them? How do we know that these miracles or divine visits are not in conflict with natural law at all?

According to Spinoza's Epistemic Theory of Miracles, there are no events that are contrary to nature. They are simply law-like events with causes and effects that we do not currently comprehend. Others claim that miracles must follow natural law because God made these natural laws in the first place. So if something doesn't follow natural law, it would seem to mean that there is no God

To take this a step further, if miracles are possible, then there must be a miracle worker. If there is a miracle worker, then there is a God. If you believe in God, then why would it be hard to then believe in miracles or the probability of divine interventions? If there is a God, then he is all powerful and omnipotent. If he created the universe, then he created the laws of nature. And if he created the laws of nature, then one can assume he must also then have the power to suspend or work outside the laws of nature. In other words, if he created it, he can change it too.

Science consists of knowledge based on the ability to observe, replicate, and explain. But when you think about it, a miracle would no longer be one if it could be explained by natural laws. Although meant to be observed, they are neither meant to be replicated nor necessarily explained. There are things in life that we are not meant to know or understand, we need only believe.

Miracles are what I like to think of as divine visits. They are supernatural, statistically impossible events that nonetheless occur. But just because they cannot be explained doesn't mean they are not real. And just because there may not appear to be a logical explanation for such events doesn't mean that they are not still taking place. Most people can pick up the Bible, Torah, or the Quran, read about certain miracles and accept it. Why then would it be so hard to accept that these divine interventions are still possible?

In my opinion, it was a modern-day miracle that started this book in the first place. In the beginning I recounted the story of Toni DiBernardo, a woman with pancreatic cancer who, after being visited in the hospital by a man whom she said looked like Jesus, was cured. It was her experience which led me to research divine interventions and write this book. Then as I neared the completion of this project, I experienced a divine intervention of my own.

When I set out to write this book, I wanted to give people hope. I wanted people to understand that miracles are not only possible and real but that they are still taking place all around us. The question of whether or not divine visits are possible is not a scientific one. Science can say that these miraculous events cannot have occurred because they would be outside the realm of natural law, but it can never prove that miracles do not exist. Science draws conclusion based on observation. So how can science draw conclusions about something it cannot see?

There are things in life that perhaps we will never be able to fully explain, but instead of trying to figure out how things happen, isn't it enough proof that they happened in the first place? As I conclude this book, I can honestly say that I am a totally different person than I was when I started it. I hope the accounts in this book have opened your heart to the power of miracles and the beauty of the divine as much as they did mine. Albert Einstein once said, "There are only two ways to live your life. One is as though nothing is a miracle. The other is as though everything is a miracle." I prefer the latter.

About the Author

Divine Visits is best-selling author Josie Varga's fifth title. She is also the author of *Visits to Heaven, Make Up Your Mind to be Happy, Visits from Heaven,* and *Footprints in the Sand: A Disabled Woman's Inspiring Journey to Happiness.* Besides being a former communications consultant, she also served as the director of communications and editor for a trade association. As a speaker, Josie helps the bereaved by sharing her message that life never ends and love never dies. She also teaches others to focus on the positive, explaining why happiness is all a matter of how we think.

She also has several other book projects in the works, including *God or Chance?*—an unparalleled book which provides mathematical and scientific statistics (based on the anthropic principle) answering the question: Was the universe the result of chance or was God or some other Supreme Being responsible?

In addition to her book writing, she has completed several treatments for reality television and is working on a pilot based on her book *Visits from Heaven.* She also has a popular group on Facebook based on *Visits from Heaven,* which provides a forum for people to share their experiences and know that life never ends and love never dies. To join or for more information, please visit:

https://www.facebookay.com/#!/groups/256369014386004/.

A creative thinker, Josie is the holder of two patents. She lives in Westfield, New Jersey, with her husband and two daughters.

Her books are available online or wherever books are sold. For more information about the author, please visit her Web site: www.josievarga.com or her blog: http://josievarga.wordpress.com/.

4TH DIMENSION PRESS

An Imprint of A.R.E. Press

4th Dimension Press is an imprint of A.R.E. Press, the publishing division of Edgar Cayce's Association for Research and Enlightenment (A.R.E.).

We publish books, DVDs, and CDs in the fields of intuition, psychic abilities, ancient mysteries, philosophy, comparative religious studies, personal and spiritual development, and holistic health.

For more information, or to receive a catalog, contact us by mail, phone, or online at:

4th Dimension Press
215 67th Street
Virginia Beach, VA 23451-2061
800-333-4499

4THDIMENSIONPRESS.COM

Who Was Edgar Cayce?
Twentieth Century Psychic and Medical Clairvoyant

Edgar Cayce (pronounced Kay-Cee, 1877-1945) has been called the "sleeping prophet," the "father of holistic medicine," and the most-documented psychic of the 20th century. For more than 40 years of his adult life, Cayce gave psychic "readings" to thousands of seekers while in an unconscious state, diagnosing illnesses and revealing lives lived in the past and prophecies yet to come. But who, exactly, was Edgar Cayce?

Cayce was born on a farm in Hopkinsville, Kentucky, in 1877, and his psychic abilities began to appear as early as his childhood. He was able to see and talk to his late grandfather's spirit, and often played with "imaginary friends" whom he said were spirits on the other side. He also displayed an uncanny ability to memorize the pages of a book simply by sleeping on it. These gifts labeled the young Cayce as strange, but all Cayce really wanted was to help others, especially children.

Later in life, Cayce would find that he had the ability to put himself into a sleep-like state by lying down on a couch, closing his eyes, and folding his hands over his stomach. In this state of relaxation and meditation, he was able to place his mind in contact with all time and space—the universal consciousness, also known as the super-conscious mind. From there, he could respond to questions as broad as, "What are the secrets of the universe?" and "What is my purpose in life?" to as specific as, "What can I do to help my arthritis?" and "How were the pyramids of Egypt built?" His responses to these questions came to be called "readings," and their insights offer practical help and advice to individuals even today.

The majority of Edgar Cayce's readings deal with holistic health and the treatment of illness. Yet, although best known for this material, the sleeping Cayce did not seem to be limited to concerns about the physical body. In fact, in their entirety, the readings discuss an astonishing 10,000 different topics. This vast array of subject matter can be narrowed down into a smaller group of topics that, when compiled together, deal with the following five categories: (1) Health-Related Information; (2) Philosophy and Reincarnation; (3) Dreams and Dream Interpretation; (4) ESP and Psychic Phenomena; and (5) Spiritual Growth, Meditation, and Prayer.

Learn more at EdgarCayce.org.

What Is A.R.E.?

Edgar Cayce founded the non-profit Association for Research and Enlightenment (A.R.E.) in 1931, to explore spirituality, holistic health, intuition, dream interpretation, psychic development, reincarnation, and ancient mysteries—all subjects that frequently came up in the more than 14,000 documented psychic readings given by Cayce.

The Mission of the A.R.E. is to help people transform their lives for the better, through research, education, and application of core concepts found in the Edgar Cayce readings and kindred materials that seek to manifest the love of God and all people and promote the purposefulness of life, the oneness of God, the spiritual nature of humankind, and the connection of body, mind, and spirit.

With an international headquarters in Virginia Beach, Va., a regional headquarters in Houston, regional representatives throughout the U.S., Edgar Cayce Centers in more than thirty countries, and individual members in more than seventy countries, the A.R.E. community is a global network of individuals.

A.R.E. conferences, international tours, camps for children and adults, regional activities, and study groups allow like-minded people to gather for educational and fellowship opportunities worldwide.

A.R.E. offers membership benefits and services that include a quarterly body-mind-spirit member magazine, *Venture Inward*, a member newsletter covering the major topics of the readings, and access to the entire set of readings in an exclusive online database.

Learn more at EdgarCayce.org.

EDGARCAYCE.ORG